Good Food, Fast

Tasty meals in 30 minutes or less

D*a*IRY COOKBOOK

Executive editor	Nick Rowe
Managing editor	Emily Anderson
Editor	Emma Callery
Designer	Graham Meigh
Proof reader	Aune Butt
Indexer	Christine Bernstein
Photographers	Steve Lee 10-2, 22, 24-29, 42-45, 47, 52-56, 59, 66, 76, 88, 97, 98-116, 118, 119, 121, 122, 124-132, 135, 138, 141, 145, 149-169.
	Steve Baxter 23, 34, 41, 68, 91, 133, 142, 143; Peter Cassidy 140; Jean Cazals 86; Jonathan Gregson 75, 136, 137; Will Heap 50; Richard Jung 61, 62; Gareth Morgans 35, 36, 58, 73, 79,82, 90, 93, 95; Lis Parsons 39, 65, 69-72, 94; Craig Robertson 31, 32, 37, 40, 49, 85; Deidre Rooney 120; Maja Smend 146; Lucinda Symons 123; Peter Thiedeke 21, 51, 78, 87; Stuart West 46, 81; Kate Whitaker 117.
Food stylist	Sara Lewis
Props stylist	Jo Harris
Recipes created by	Pat Alburey, Kate Belcher, Angela Boggiano, Matthew Drennan, Silvana Franco, Alice Hart, Kathryn Hawkins, Sal Henley, Diana Henry, Ghillie James, Lizzie Kamenetzky, Lucy Knox, Debbie Major, Sue McMahon, Kim Morphew, Tom Norrington-Davies, Glen Smith, Lucy Williams, Mitzie Wilson
Nutritional consultant	Dr Wendy Doyle
Recipe testers	Leah Figiel, Carolyn Glazebrook, Katy Hackforth, Chris Perry, Sian Stark
Production	Priti Kothary

With special thanks to delicious. MAGAZINE

Eaglemoss Consumer Publications Ltd

Electra House, Electra Way, Crewe, Cheshire, CW1 6WZ

Telephone 01270 270050 Website www.dairydiary.co.uk

First printed March 2010

© Eaglemoss Consumer Publications Ltd

ISBN-13: 978-0-9560894-1-0

123456789

Contents

Cooking should be a pleasure not a chore, but that can be hard to achieve when you are short of time and hungry people are patrolling the kitchen. Good food doesn't have to come with fancy sauces and flashy presentation: the simplest meal can be truly delicious.

To cook good food, fast, you need the right ingredients. In addition to storecupboard basics, that means a freezer stocked with a few corner-cutting ingredients. Chillies, ginger, cheese, herbs and breadcrumbs can be frozen, chopped or grated, in wraps of cling film or small bags so that all you need to do is unpeel the plastic and use them.

Frozen vegetables are just as nutritious as fresh, and far more convenient to use if you've had a busy day or have had to change your plans and didn't have time to get to a shop. Freezing meat already cut up into chunks will defrost more quickly and save you time when you cook. Frozen stocks are often of higher quality than the dried variety, too – and a good stock can really lift a meal, bringing richness and more complex flavours.

Organisation

It is easier to cook when everything is to hand. So gather together your equipment before you start cooking and keep it on the counter, only to return to the cupboard when you are clearing up. Read the recipe through and also get all the ingredients together before you start cooking. One advantage of this is that meat will cook faster from room temperature than straight from the fridge.

While you are cooking, set one large bowl aside for scraps and peelings. This will make tidying up much faster, especially if you clean other surfaces as you go along. Have a bowl of hot soapy water to rinse pots straight after use, and put other crockery straight into the dishwasher. It's always rather pleasing to serve up knowing that the washing up is already organised. If the recipe features a sauce that might need reducing, cook it in a large skillet so that the liquid evaporates faster.

Armed with these simple tips, you are now ready to cook good food, fast – and when we say fast, we mean fast: no recipe in this book takes longer than 30 minutes to prepare and cook. So whether you are looking for a snack, main course or dessert, the choice is yours.

Pre-cooked or pre-cut vegetables are a time saver, as is ready marinated meat or fish.

Cook and freeze sauces and stocks for use later. Before emptying leftover portions into the bin, think if they could be re-used. For example, vegetable purées are fantastically flavoursome thickeners for soups, sauces and casseroles.

Think ahead: if you double or even triple the quantities, you can cook once and eat twice or three times by chilling or freezing the extra food – so you have a bank of meals that just need re-heating rather than cooking.

Cook's information

Dry weight conversions

Recommended grams (g)	Imperial ounces (oz)
15	½
25	1
50	2
75	3
110	4 (¼lb)
150	5
175	6
200	7
225	8 (½lb)
250	9
275	10
300	11
350	12 (¾lb)
375	13
400	14
425	15
450	16 (1lb)
500	1lb 2oz
680	1½lb
750	1lb 10oz
900	2lb

These quantities are not exact, but they have been calculated to give proportionately correct measurements.

Liquid conversions

Metric (ml)	Imperial (fl oz)	US cups
15	½	1 tbsp (level)
30	1	⅛
60	2	¼
90	3	⅜
125	4	½
150	5 (¼ pint)	⅔
175	6	¾
225	8	1
300	10 (½ pint)	1¼
350	12	1½
450	16	2
500	18	2¼
600	20 (1 pint)	2½
900	1½ pints	3¾
1 litre	1¾ pints	1 quart (4 cups)
1.25 litres	2 pints	1¼ quarts
1.5 litres	2½ pints	3 US pints
2 litres	3½ pints	2 quarts

568ml = 1 UK pint   (20fl oz)   16fl oz = 1 US pint

These quantities are not exact, but they have been calculated to give proportionately correct measurements.

Oven temperatures

°C	°F	Gas mark	Description
110	225	¼	cool
120/130	250	½	cool
140	275	1	very low
150	300	2	very low
160/170	325	3	low to moderate
180	350	4	moderate
190	375	5	moderately hot
200	400	6	hot
220	425	7	hot
230	450	8	hot
240	475	9	very hot

Guide to recommended equivalent settings, not exact conversions. Always refer to your cooker instruction book.

Grilling times: fish

Type of fish	Grilling time
Cod (steak)	5–6 min each side
Dover sole (whole)	4–6 min each side
Dover sole (fillet)	2–3 min each side
Halibut (steak)	5–6 min each side
Herring (whole)	4–5 min each side
Mackerel (whole)	6–7 min each side
Monkfish (steak)	5–6 min each side
Plaice (whole)	4–6 min each side
Plaice (fillet)	2–3 min each side
Salmon (steak)	5–6 min each side
Tuna (steak)	1–2 min each side

Times given for fish weighing approximately 175–225g (6–8oz).

Guideline daily amounts: adults

	Women	Men
Energy (calories)	2,000	2,500
Fat (g)	70	95
Saturated fat (g)	20	30
Carbohydrate (g)	230	300
Total sugars (g)	90	120
Protein (g)	45	55
Dietary fibre (g)	24	24
Salt (g)	6	6

Suitable for vegetarians

If you are cooking for a vegetarian, please ensure that any cheese, yogurt or pesto sauce you use is suitable for vegetarians. It should give this information on the jar or packet

Roasting times: meat

Set oven temperature to 180°C/350°F/Gas 4.

	Cooking time per 450g/1lb	Extra cooking time
Beef		
Rare	20 min	20 min
Medium	25 min	25 min
Well done	30 min	30 min
Lamb		
Medium	25 min	25 min
Well done	30 min	30 min
Pork		
Medium	30 min	30 min
Well done	35 min	35 min

Let the cooked meat rest for 5–15 minutes before carving to allow the juices to be reabsorbed and to make carving easier.

Steaming times: vegetables

Vegetable	Steaming time
Asparagus	5–7 min
Beansprouts	3–4 min
Beetroot (sliced)	5–7 min
Broccoli (florets)	5–7 min
Brussels sprouts	5–7 min
Cabbage (chopped)	4–6 min
Cauliflower (florets)	5–7 min
Carrots (thickly sliced)	5–7 min
Courgettes (sliced)	3–5 min
Green beans	5–7 min
Leeks	5–8 min
Mangetout peas	3–5 min
Peas	3–5 min
Potatoes (cubed)	5–7 min

Times given are for steaming from when water has started to boil.

Roasting times: poultry

	Oven temperature	Cooking time	Extra per 450g/1lb	Resting cooking time
Chicken	200°C/400°F/Gas 6	20 min	30 min	15 min
Turkey (stuffed weight)				
small (under 6kg/13lb)	200°C/400°F/Gas 6	12 min	20 min	30 min
large	180°C/350°F/Gas 4	16 min	—	30 min
Duck	200°C/400°F/Gas 6 for 45 min then 180°C/350°F/Gas 4	35 min	—	15 min

Speedy soup

For classic comfort food or classy starters these soups are perfect all year round.

Adding the bicarbonate of soda helps to neutralise the acidity of the canned tomatoes and will help to prevent the crème fraîche from curdling as it is stirred into the soup.

12

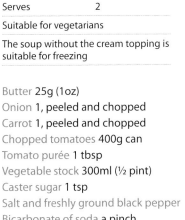

Time	30 minutes
Calories per portion	286 Kcal
Fat per portion	19g
of which saturated	10.9g
Serves	2
Suitable for vegetarians	
The soup without the cream topping is suitable for freezing	

Butter 25g (1oz)
Onion 1, peeled and chopped
Carrot 1, peeled and chopped
Chopped tomatoes 400g can
Tomato purée 1 tbsp
Vegetable stock 300ml (½ pint)
Caster sugar 1 tsp
Salt and freshly ground black pepper
Bicarbonate of soda a pinch
Green pesto sauce 1 tbsp
Crème fraîche 2 tbsp

Tomato soup with pesto cream

This soup is so rich and tasty you will never want to have canned tomato soup again.

Melt the butter in a saucepan and add the onion and carrot. Cook over a medium heat for 5–7 minutes, until the vegetables have softened, stirring occasionally.

Add the chopped tomatoes, tomato purée, vegetable stock and caster sugar to the pan and bring to the boil. Then reduce the heat, cover the pan and simmer the soup for 10–15 minutes, until the vegetables are really tender.

Remove the pan from the heat and purée the soup using a hand-held electric wand or in a food processor or blender. Return to the pan, if necessary, season the soup to taste and stir in the bicarbonate of soda, which may fizz slightly, but stir until the fizzing stops.

Stir the pesto into the crème fraiche. Heat the soup and then pour it into warm bowls. Spoon the pesto crème fraîche on top, swirling it into the soup and serve immediately.

30

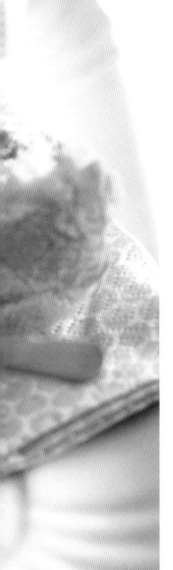

SPEEDY SOUP

Time	20 minutes
Calories per portion	161 Kcal
Fat per portion	6g
of which saturated	1g
Serves	2
Suitable for vegetarians	
Suitable for freezing	

Vegetable stock 600ml (1 pint)
Bay leaf 1
Leek 1, trimmed, split lengthways and finely shredded
Courgette 1, trimmed and diced
Broccoli 110g (4oz), trimmed and cut into small florets
Asparagus spears 6, woody ends removed and cut into 2.5cm (1in) lengths
French beans 75g (3oz), trimmed and cut into 2.5cm (1in) lengths
Cornflour 1 tbsp
Salt and freshly ground black pepper
Basil leaves a small handful
Green pesto sauce 2 tbsp

Spring vegetable potage

A vibrant and healthy soup full of the best flavours of the season.

Pour the vegetable stock into a large saucepan, add the bay leaf and bring the stock to the boil. Then add all the vegetables, cover the pan and simmer for 7–8 minutes, until just tender.

Blend the cornflour with 2 tablespoons of cold water and stir into the vegetables. Bring back to the boil, stirring, and cook for 1 minute, until slightly thickened. Discard the bay leaf and season to taste. Shred all but a few basil leaves, and stir into the soup.

Ladle into warm bowls and top each with a dollop of pesto sauce. Serve immediately sprinkled with remaining basil leaves.

Replace any of the vegetables with alternatives or add diced cooked chicken or peeled prawns to the vegetables when you add the cornflour paste, and heat through until hot.

Thai green curry paste is a fragrant blend of garlic, ginger, lime leaves, lemon grass and spices, or use a mild Indian curry paste.

Time	25 minutes
Calories per portion	296 Kcal
Fat per portion	20g
of which saturated	11.5g
Serves	2
Suitable for vegetarians	
Suitable for freezing	

Vegetable oil 1 tbsp
Spring onions 1 bunch, trimmed and finely chopped
Thai green curry paste 1 tbsp
Potatoes 2, peeled and cut into small chunks
Vegetable stock 450ml (¾ pint)
Canned coconut milk 150ml (¼ pint)
Baby spinach 110g (4oz)
Coriander small bunch, chopped, reserving a few leaves to garnish
Salt and freshly ground black pepper

Thai spinach and potato soup

Bring a taste of the Orient to the table with this simple, yet exotically flavoured, bowl of ingredients.

Heat the oil in a medium saucepan and stir-fry the spring onions for 1 minute. Add the curry paste and cook for a further minute.

Add the potatoes and cook, stirring, for another minute. Then pour the vegetable stock and coconut milk into the pan and bring to the boil. Half cover the pan and let it simmer for 10–12 minutes, until the potatoes are tender.

Meanwhile, trim and roughly chop the spinach. Reserving a few coriander leaves for garnish, roughly chop the rest.

Stir the spinach and chopped coriander into the soup ingredients and heat through for 2–3 minutes, stirring, until the spinach is wilted. Season to taste.

Ladle into warm bowls and garnish with the reserved coriander leaves to serve.

Time	25 minutes
Calories per portion	99 Kcal
Fat per portion	1g
of which saturated	0.1g
Serves	3
Suitable for vegetarians	
Suitable for freezing without the yogurt	

Carrot 1 large, peeled and cut into small pieces
Celeriac, ¼ bulb, peeled and flesh cut into small pieces
Onion 1, peeled and chopped
Vegetable stock 600ml (1 pint)
Eating apples 2
Salt and freshly ground black pepper
Grated nutmeg a pinch
Low fat natural yogurt 2–3 tbsp
Ready made croutons to serve

Carrot, apple and celeriac soup

Packed full of flavour and low in calories here is a tasty soup to hit the spot when you fancy a light snack.

Put the vegetables in a medium saucepan and pour over the vegetable stock and bring to the boil. Then reduce the heat, cover the pan and simmer the soup for 5 minutes.

Meanwhile, peel, core and chop the apples. Stir into the vegetables and continue to simmer for a further 5 minutes until tender.

Remove the pan from the heat and blend the soup using a hand-held electric wand or in a food processor or blender until the vegetables are finely chopped. Return to the pan, if necessary, season to taste and add the nutmeg.

Stir in the yogurt and heat through very gently for 1–2 minutes without boiling, until piping hot. Ladle into warm bowls and top each with a handful of croutons and a grinding of black pepper.

25

Celeriac is a knobbly root vegetable related to celery. If unavailable, use 2 sticks chopped celery instead.

If you like spicy food, add a freshly chopped chilli to the ingredients. Sauté it at the same time as the onion and celery.

Time	25 minutes
Calories per portion	280 Kcal
Fat per portion	12.6g
of which saturated	6.6g
Serves	2
Suitable for vegetarians	
Suitable for freezing	

Butter 25g (1oz)
Onion 1, peeled and chopped
Celery 2 sticks, sliced
Red pepper 1, deseeded and chopped
Chilli powder 1 tsp
Chopped tomatoes 400g can
Red kidney beans 220g can, drained
Vegetable stock cube 1, crumbled
Black treacle 1 tbsp
Salt and freshly ground black pepper

Chilli bean soup

This filling, mildly spicy main-meal soup is perfect for cold days.

Melt the butter in a saucepan and add the onion and celery and cook over a medium heat for 4–5 minutes, until the vegetables start to soften. Then add the red pepper to the pan and cook for a further 2–3 minutes. Add the chilli powder and cook for about 1 minute.

Add the tomatoes, kidney beans, stock cube, treacle and 175ml (6fl oz) water to the pan and bring to the boil. Then reduce the heat, cover the pan and simmer the soup for 10–15 minutes, adjusting with some extra water if necessary. Season the soup to taste just before serving and ladle into warm bowls.

Time	20 minutes
Calories per portion	471 Kcal
Fat per portion	39.4g
of which saturated	2g
Serves	2
Suitable for vegetarians	
Suitable for freezing	

Vegetable oil **1 tbsp**
Onion **1, peeled and chopped**
Vegetable stock **600ml (1 pint)**
Broccoli **250g (9oz), trimmed and cut into small florets**
Blue cheese **110g (4oz)**
Salt and freshly ground black pepper
Parsley **a few sprigs, finely chopped**
Double cream **2 tbsp**

Freeze any leftover blue cheese, crumbled into small quantities ready for adding to soups and pies straight from frozen.

Broccoli and blue cheese soup

This is a rich and flavoursome soup that is also a good way of using up leftover blue cheese.

Heat the oil in a medium saucepan and gently fry the onion for 5 minutes, stirring, until it has softened but not browned. Pour the vegetable stock over the onion, bring it to the boil and then add the broccoli

Reduce the heat, cover the pan and simmer the soup for 6–7 minutes, until tender. Remove from the heat.

Blend the soup with a hand-held electric wand, food processor or blender until the broccoli is finely chopped. If necessary, return to the pan, crumble the cheese into the soup, reserving some to garnish, and stir in. Return to the heat and cook very gently, stirring, for 2–3 minutes until the cheese has melted and the soup is piping hot. Season to taste.

Ladle into warm soup bowls, crumble over the remaining cheese, sprinkle with chopped parsley and add a swirl of cream.

For a more authentic dish, use fine egg noodles instead of spaghetti.

Time	15 minutes
Calories per portion	415 Kcal
Fat per portion	3.3g
of which saturated	0.6g
Serves	2
Suitable for freezing	

Chicken stock 600ml (1 pint)
Skinless chicken breasts 2, thinly sliced
Quick cook spaghetti 75g, uncooked and broken into short lengths
Butter beans 410g can, drained and rinsed
Cherry tomatoes a good handful, halved
Red chilli deseeded and finely sliced
Salt and freshly ground black pepper
Parsley a handful, chopped

Chicken, pasta and butter bean ramen

Ramen is a type of noodle used in Japanese cooking; here spaghetti has been used in its place.

Bring the chicken stock to the boil in a large saucepan over a medium heat, then add the chicken breasts and spaghetti. Simmer, partially covered, for 5 minutes.

Stir in the butter beans, cherry tomatoes and red chilli and simmer for 2–3 minutes, until the chicken and spaghetti are cooked. Season and stir in the parsley.

Divide between deep bowls and serve with crusty bread

Choose a floury type of potato (one good for mashing), which will help to make this a very smooth soup.

Time	30 minutes
Calories per portion	279 Kcal
Fat per portion	19g
of which saturated	10.1g
Serves	2
Suitable for freezing	

Butter 25g (1oz)
Onion 1 small, peeled and chopped
Leek 1 small, trimmed and sliced
Streaky bacon 4 rashers, chopped
Potato 1, peeled and cubed
Ham or vegetable stock 300ml
(½ pint)
Milk 150ml (¼ pint)
Salt and freshly ground black
pepper

Bacon, leek and potato soup

It's no wonder that this is a classic flavour combination – they all blend perfectly together.

Melt the butter in a saucepan and add the onion and leek and cook over a medium heat for about 5 minutes, stirring occasionally. Add the most of the bacon, reserving the rest for garnish, to the pan and cook for a further 2–3 minutes. Then add the potato and cook for 1–2 minutes until the potato is coated in the butter.

Pour the ham or vegetable stock into the pan and bring the mixture to the boil. Then reduce the heat, cover the pan and simmer the soup for 12–15 minutes, or until the potato is tender.

Remove the pan from the heat and purée the soup using a hand-held electric wand or in a food processor or blender. If necessary, pour the soup back into the saucepan. Add the milk, adjusting with some water if necessary. Check for seasoning and then reheat gently before serving with the remaining chopped bacon.

Time	30 minutes
Calories per portion	275 Kcal
Fat per portion	12.1g
of which saturated	3.7g
Serves	6

Olive oil 2 tbsp
Butter 15g (½oz)
Onion 1 large, chopped
Garlic 1 clove, peeled and finely chopped
Floury potato 1 large, cubed
Chicken stock 1.5 litres (2½ pints)
Frozen peas 900g (2lb)
Watercress 100g bag
Salt and freshly ground black pepper
Pancetta or thin rashers smoked streaky bacon 75g (3oz), chopped

Winter pea and watercress soup with crispy pancetta

The peppery, sweet soup contrasts wonderfully with the salty pancetta.

Heat the oil and butter in a large saucepan, add the onion and garlic and cook gently for 5 minutes, until beginning to soften. Add the potato and toss with the onion and garlic, then pour in the chicken stock and bring to the boil. Reduce the heat, cover the pan and simmer the soup for 15 minutes, until the potato is tender.

Add the frozen peas and simmer for 3 minutes. Then add the watercress and stir in until wilted. Remove from the heat, let it cool for a few minutes then purée with a hand-held electric wand or in a food processor or blender, until smooth. Return to the pan, if necessary, season to taste and keep warm over a gentle heat.

Meanwhile, preheat the grill to hot. Grill the pancetta or bacon for 2–3 minutes on each side, until crisp. Remove and drain on kitchen paper and then break up into pieces.

Ladle the soup into warm bowls and top each with some of the pancetta pieces.

Pancetta is cured pork and is usually sold ready-chopped near to the bacon in the supermarket.

Time	30 minutes
Calories per portion	202 Kcal
Fat per portion	14g
of which saturated	6.9g
Serves	3

Butter 25g (1oz)
Onion 1, peeled and chopped
Chorizo 75g (3oz), sliced
Potato 1, peeled and cubed
Garlic 1 clove, peeled and crushed
Ham or vegetable stock 600ml (1 pint)
Kale 50g (2oz), finely shredded
Salt and freshly ground black pepper

Chorizo and kale soup

With the addition of fresh kale, this Spanish-influenced soup is packed full of vitamins.

Melt the butter in a large saucepan and add the onion. Cook over a medium heat for 4–5 minutes until the onion starts to soften, then add the chorizo, potato and garlic and cook for a further 1–2 minutes.

Pour the ham or vegetable stock into the pan and bring to the boil. Then reduce the heat, cover the pan and simmer the soup for 12–15 minutes until the potato is tender. Use a potato masher to mash some of the potato to thicken the soup.

Add the kale to the pan, and then simmer, uncovered for 2–3 minutes, until the kale is tender. Season to taste before serving.

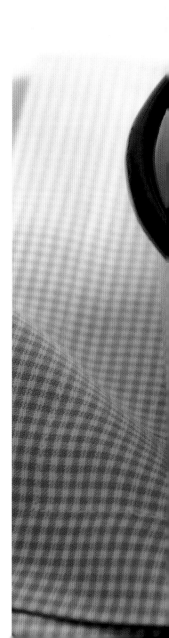

You could slice a complete sausage or ring of chorizo rather than buying it ready-sliced.

Quick fixes

These dishes will help keep you on the move, however little time you have.

Take care not to overcook the eggs as they will become dry – they should be softly set and still shiny.

28

Time	25 minutes
Calories per portion	748 Kcal
Fat per portion	44g
of which saturated	11.2g
Serves	3
Suitable for vegetarians	

Olive oil 2 tbsp
Red pepper 1 small, deseeded and cut into thin strips
Green pepper 1 small, deseeded and cut into thin strips
Spring onions 3 large, trimmed and cut into thin slices, diagonally
Sun-dried tomatoes in olive oil 6, drained and roughly chopped
Eggs 6
Salt and freshly ground black pepper
Butter 25g (1oz)
Soft flour tortillas 4, warmed

For the salad
Avocado 1 small, stoned, peeled and cut into slices
Tomato 1 large, cut into wedges
Crisp lettuce 4–6 leaves, torn
Rice wine vinegar 1 tbsp

Mexican-style scrambled eggs

Late home from work and famished? Mexican-inspired scrambled eggs wrapped in tortillas are just the job.

Heat the olive oil in a large frying pan, preferably non-stick. Add the peppers and cook gently for 5 minutes, until softened. Then add the spring onions and sun-dried tomatoes and heat through.

Meanwhile, put all the salad ingredients into a bowl and toss gently together.

Beat the eggs in a separate bowl and lightly season. Remove the vegetables from the frying pan on to a plate and add the butter to the pan. Allow it to melt until sizzling hot, and then mix in the eggs and stir gently, but quickly until the eggs are lightly scrambled.

To serve, spoon the vegetables on to the wraps and divide the scrambled eggs over the top. Roll up and serve immediately, accompanied with the avocado salad.

Time	30 minutes
Calories per portion	561 Kcal
Fat per portion	42.8g
of which saturated	16.8g
Serves	4
Suitable for vegetarians	

Olive oil 4 tbsp
Butter 25g (1oz)
Waxy potatoes 2 large (about 500g/1lb 2oz), peeled and finely sliced
Closed cup mushrooms 250g (9oz), wiped and finely sliced
Garlic 4 cloves, peeled and crushed
Salt and freshly ground black pepper
Chives 25g (1oz), snipped
Eggs 8, separated
Camembert or Brie 110g (4oz), chopped

Oozy mushroom rolled omelettes

Here is a luscious light omelette that tastes very indulgent.

Heat the oil and half the butter in a frying pan over a medium heat. Add the potato to the pan and cook for 6–8 minutes, turning, until tender and golden. Remove and set aside in a bowl.

Add the mushrooms to the pan and toss well in the pan juices for 3–4 minutes, until tender. Add the garlic and cook for a further minute, then season. Remove from the pan and toss with the potatoes and most of the chives.

Put the egg whites into a large bowl and whisk until soft peaks form. Gently beat the egg yolks in a separate bowl, then fold into the egg whites until completely mixed.

Heat half the remaining butter in the pan over a high heat and, when melted, add half the eggs. Lower the heat and cook for 2–3 minutes, until the underside is just set and golden.

Sprinkle half of the omelette with half the cheese and add half the potatoes and mushrooms. Flip over the other half of the omelette and remove from the heat. Keep warm while repeating to make the other omelette.

Sprinkle the omelettes with the remaining chives. Halve each one and divide between four warm serving plates. Serve with slices of griddled bread.

Replace the garlic and chives with a bunch of finely sliced spring onions, and the Camembert with grated Cheddar, if you like.

31

To help keep the white of the poached eggs from dispersing too widely in the water, add 1 tablespoon of white wine vinegar as the water comes to the boil.

Time	20 minutes
Calories per portion	440 Kcal
Fat per portion	22g
of which saturated	3.9g
Serves	2
Suitable for vegetarians	

Puy lentils 250g (9oz)
Red onion 1, peeled and cut into 8 wedges
Baby leeks 200g (7oz), trimmed
Olive oil 2 tbsp
Salt and freshly ground black pepper
Lemon 1, juice only
Wholegrain mustard 1 tsp
Chopped flatleaf parsley 2 tbsp, plus extra for garnishing
SunBlush tomatoes 50g (2oz), drained and roughly chopped
Eggs 2

Puy lentil salad with griddled leeks and poached egg

A super-quick warm salad that has a wonderful combination of textures and flavours.

Warm the Puy lentils in a saucepan with a splash of water.

Place a griddle pan over a high heat. Put the onion, baby leeks, ½ tablespoon of the olive oil and plenty of seasoning in a bowl. Turn to coat in the oil and then spread out in the hot griddle pan in a single layer and cook for 1–2 minutes on each side, until marked with griddle lines. The leeks will cook faster than the onions. Remove to a plate with tongs.

Combine the remaining olive oil with the lemon juice, wholegrain mustard and parsley. Stir into the warm lentils with the SunBlush tomatoes and the griddled vegetables.

Bring a pan of water to a gentle boil. Then, one by one, crack each egg into a small bowl and pour into the water, scooping the white towards the yolk. Poach each egg for 2–4 minutes, depending on how you like the yolk.

Serve the eggs on top of the lentil salad and sprinkle with the remaining chopped parsley.

20

Choose a rich and creamy goat's cheese to contrast with the texture of the rice and beans.

15

Time	15 minutes
Calories per portion	598 Kcal
Fat per portion	19g
of which saturated	10.5g
Serves	2
Suitable for vegetarians	

Basmati rice 150g (5oz), rinsed
Mixed bean salad 420g can, drained and rinsed
Flatleaf parsley a handful, chopped
Red onion ½, peeled and diced
Cherry tomatoes 150g (5oz), quartered
Sun-dried tomatoes in olive oil 2, drained and roughly chopped
Garlic 1 clove, peeled and crushed
Lemon ½, for squeezing
Salt and freshly ground black pepper
Goat's cheese 2 thick slices

Bean and rice salad with goat's cheese

The perfect convenience food, but with plenty of taste and goodness.

Put the rice in a pan and cover with double the amount of water, bring to the boil. Turn down the heat, cover and leave to simmer for 10 minutes, until the rice is just cooked. Rinse in a sieve under cold water to cool down the rice.

Place the mixed bean salad in a large bowl and mix with the basmati rice. Then add the parsley, red onion, cherry tomatoes and sun-dried tomatoes.

Dress with 2 tablespoons of olive oil from the tomato jar and the garlic and then squeeze over the lemon juice. Season well and toss.

Divide between plates, top each with a thick slice of the goat's cheese and drizzle with extra oil (again from the tomato jar).

Time	20 minutes
Calories per portion	628 Kcal
Fat per portion	37g
of which saturated	11.5g
Serves	3
Suitable for vegetarians	

Bulgar wheat 200g (7oz)
Lemons 2, finely grated zest and
juice of 1, the other cut into wedges
to serve
Young leaf spinach 150g (5oz)
Boiling water 600ml (1 pint)
Artichoke antipasto 285g jar,
drained but reserve 2 tbsp oil
Cherry tomatoes 250g (9oz), halved
Feta cheese 200g (7oz)
Salt and freshly ground black
pepper

Feta, artichoke and tomato bulgar wheat

An East-meets-West salad fit for a summer's day.

Put the bulgar wheat into a large bowl, add the lemon zest and spinach leaves. Pour over the boiling water, stir and cover with cling film. Set aside for 15 minutes, or until the bulgar wheat has softened but still has a slight bite. Drain in a sieve, squeezing out the excess liquid well. Return to the bowl.

Halve the artichokes and add to the bowl, along with the cherry tomatoes and crumble over the feta. Drizzle with the reserved oil and season to taste with the lemon juice and salt and freshly ground black pepper.

Gently toss together with the bulgar wheat and divide between wide bowls. Serve with the lemon wedges.

QUICK FIXES

20:

Use couscous instead of bulgar wheat if you prefer. Just follow the instructions on the packet for how to cook.

Time	10 minutes
Calories per portion	510 Kcal
Fat per portion	45g
of which saturated	6.6g
Serves	2

Watercress, rocket and spinach
salad 135g bag
Avocado 1, stoned, peeled and
sliced
Toasted pine nuts 30g (1¼oz)
Cooked crispy bacon 40g (1½oz),
broken up
Crab meat 110g (4oz) fresh or
170g can white crab meat in brine,
drained
Olive oil 3 tbsp
Lemon juice 1 tbsp
Salt and freshly ground black
pepper

Crab, avocado and bacon salad

*A whole variety of different textures and delicious
flavours packed into one dish.*

Divide the salad leaves between two large serving plates. Scatter
over the avocado, toasted pine nuts and crispy bacon and then top
with the crab meat.

Whisk together the olive oil and lemon juice in a small bowl. Season
to taste and drizzle over the salad to serve.

*To cook crispy bacon, use
4 rashers of thinly sliced
bacon and grill on high
for 10 minutes.*

Sun-dried tomato paste has a lovely flavour and can be used in place of tomato purée in sauces or for spreading on sandwiches and pizzas.

Time	15 minutes
Cooking time	2 minutes
Calories per portion	425 Kcal
Fat per portion	17g
of which saturated	2.6g
Serves	4

Cannellini beans 400g can or jar, drained and rinsed
Tuna in olive oil 300g can, drained and flaked into large chunks
Red onion 1 small, peeled and finely sliced
Cherry tomatoes 12, halved
Flatleaf parsley a large handful, chopped
Olive oil 3 tbsp
Lemons 2 small, juice of 1 and the other cut into wedges
Dijon mustard 1 tsp
Garlic 1 clove, peeled and crushed
Sourdough or rye bread 4 thick slices
Sun-dried tomato paste 3 tbsp

Tuna and cannellini beans on griddled tomato bread

This cracking combination is especially successful if you can buy good quality tuna.

Mix together the beans, tuna, red onion, tomatoes and parsley in a large bowl.

In another bowl, whisk together 2 tablespoons of the oil, the lemon juice and the mustard and garlic. Season, pour over the tuna and beans and toss together well.

Heat a griddle pan until very hot. Brush the bread on both sides with the remaining oil and griddle for 1 minute on each side, until golden with charred lines.

Spread one side of each slice of bread with the tomato paste. Pile on the beans and tuna and serve with the remaining lemon, cut into wedges, to squeeze over.

Time	25 minutes
Calories per portion	325 Kcal
Fat per portion	13.6g
of which saturated	7.5g
Serves	4

Skinless chicken breasts 4 large, cut into strips about
1cm (½in) thick
Peanut or satay cooking sauce 150-200g (5-7oz)
Coconut milk 175ml (6fl oz)
Lime 1, grated zest and juice of ½ and the rest cut into wedges
Mixed vegetable stir-fry 350g pack

Chicken satay with Indonesian-style salad

Succulent, nutty chicken served with a bowl of crunchy finely chopped vegetables.

Toss the chicken strips in half of the peanut cooking sauce in a bowl and set aside to marinate for 10 minutes.

Meanwhile, soak 12 medium-length wooden skewers in hot water. Preheat the grill to hot and line a baking tray with foil.

Thread the chicken onto the drained skewers (2–3 strips on each) and lay on the tray. Grill for 8–10 minutes, turning halfway, until lightly charred and cooked through.

Meanwhile, put the remaining peanut cooking sauce in a saucepan with the coconut milk and lime zest. Place over a medium heat and simmer for 5 minutes. Then stir in the lime juice and set aside to cool and thicken slightly.

Divide the uncooked mixed vegetable stir-fry between four bowls and serve alongside the chicken satay skewers and lime wedges. Drizzle some warm peanut sauce over each salad and serve the rest in bowls for dipping the satay in.

Some supermarkets sell a 165ml mini can of coconut milk, which is ideal for this recipe. Otherwise, use part of a can and use the rest with Thai curry paste for another meal.

If fresh oregano is unobtainable, use a teaspoon of dried instead.

Time	15 minutes
Calories per portion	538 Kcal
Fat per portion	22g
of which saturated	11.1g
Serves	4

Lamb leg steaks 4, trimmed of their fat
Salt and freshly ground black pepper
Olive oil for drizzling
Oregano a small handful, chopped
Pitta breads 4
Tomatoes 2, sliced
Feta cheese 150g (5oz), cut into slices
Cucumber 5cm (2in), sliced
Oregano to garnish

Greek lamb pittas

Revive happy holiday memories with this easy and delicious sandwich.

Preheat the grill to hot. Place the lamb steaks between sheets of cling film and flatten with the end of a rolling pin. Season well, drizzle with some olive oil and scatter over the oregano. Cook under the grill for 6–8 minutes on each side and set aside.

Toast the pitta breads in a toaster. Split open and stuff each with the lamb, tomatoes, feta and a few slices of cucumber. Garnish with the oregano.

Time	15 minutes
Calories per portion	426 Kcal
Fat per portion	36g
of which saturated	14.9g
Serves	2

Beef sausages 4, skins removed
Chilli flakes a good pinch
Garlic and coriander mini naan breads 2–4, depending on their size
Crème fraîche 2 tbsp
Red onion ½, peeled and thinly sliced
Chopped mint leaves 2 tbsp
Rocket leaves a small handful
Olive oil to drizzle

Naan bread pizzas

A mildly spicy, scrumptious sausage dish, perfect for lunch with a friend.

Preheat the grill to medium and put a frying pan over a medium heat on the hob. Add the sausages and chilli flakes. Roughly break up the meat and cook the sausages until well browned and tender.

Place the naan breads on a baking sheet and top with the browned sausagemeat and crème fraîche. Scatter over the red onion and mint leaves and then grill for 3–4 minutes.

Top each naan with half of the the rocket leaves and a drizzle of olive oil before serving.

15

Swap the garlic naans for plain ones and top with some crumbled Cheshire cheese along with the other ingredients.

Everyday eating

Everyday shouldn't have to mean run of the mill – these recipes are refreshingly different.

The secret behind making a good omelette is to keep the heat quite low and allow the egg to cook gently so it doesn't toughen and become rubbery.

44

Time	30 minutes
Calories per portion	321 Kcal
Fat per portion	18g
of which saturated	4.2g
Serves	3
Suitable for vegetarians	

Sweet potato 1 large, peeled, cut in half lengthways and then into 5mm (¼in) slices
Vegetable oil 1 tbsp
Red pepper 1, deseeded and cut into thin slices
Garlic 2 cloves, peeled and crushed
Eggs 6, beaten
Salt and freshly ground black pepper
Finely chopped parsley 2 tbsp
Finely chopped coriander 2 tbsp

Sweet potato and pepper omelette

A colourful vegetarian dish that is just as good served hot as it is cold. It's good for a picnic, too.

Place the sweet potato in a saucepan, cover with water, bring to the boil and cook for about 5 minutes until just tender. Drain well.

Heat the oil in a medium frying pan and gently fry the pepper and garlic for about 5 minutes until softened. Add the potato slices, and cook, stirring, for a further minute.

Pack the vegetables evenly over the base of the frying pan and pour in the eggs and plenty of seasoning. Cook the omelette over a gentle heat, pushing the cooked egg from the edge of the pan into the centre, until the egg is set all over – it will take about 10 minutes to set completely.

Preheat the grill to hot, and place the omelette under the grill, protecting the frying pan handle if necessary, to cook for 2–3 minutes to lightly brown the top.

Serve hot or cold, straight from the pan, cut into wedges and sprinkled with the chopped herbs. A green salad makes a tasty crisp accompaniment.

For a version that is lighter in calories, omit the crème fraîche and add some steamed beans for textural variety.

Time	30 minutes
Calories per portion	449 Kcal
Fat per portion	13g
of which saturated	1.2g
Serves	2
Suitable for vegetarians	

Baking potatoes 2 large
Olive oil 1 tbsp, plus extra for coating the potatoes
Crushed sea salt for coating the potatoes
Onion 1, peeled and finely diced
Red pepper 1, deseeded and diced
Courgette 1, trimmed and diced
Chilli powder 1 tsp
Paprika ½ tsp
Fresh chilli bean soup 600ml pot
Coriander a handful, roughly chopped
Crème fraîche to serve

Vegetable chilli jackets

Spicy and filling – just the thing to warm your tastebuds on a blustery evening.

Preheat the oven to 200°C/Gas 6. Coat the baking potatoes with a little olive oil, prick well with a fork and then rub with the sea salt. Cook in the microwave for 10 minutes on high then bake in the oven for 20 minutes, until crispy and cooked through.

Meanwhile, heat the tablespoon of olive oil in a sauté or frying pan. Add the onion and cook over a low heat for 5 minutes, then add the red pepper and courgette. Stir in the chilli powder and paprika and cook for 8 minutes more or until softened.

Pour the chilli bean soup into the pan, bring to a simmer and then let it bubble for about 3 minutes, until thickened.

Remove the potatoes from the oven and split open. Spoon the chilli into the jackets, scatter with the coriander and top with dollops of crème fraîche.

Time	20 minutes
Calories per portion	447 Kcal
Fat per portion	20g
of which saturated	5.3g
Serves	2
Suitable for vegetarians if using a Parmesan substitute	

Olive oil 2 tbsp
Onion 1 large, peeled and roughly chopped
Middle Eastern-style spice 2 tsp
Medium curry powder 1 tsp
Chopped tomatoes 400g can
Vegetable stock cube 1
Fresh penne or similar pasta 250g (9oz)
Capers 1–2 tbsp
Grated Parmesan cheese 4 tbsp

East/West pasta

Fed up with traditional-style pasta dishes? This spicy combination of ingredients is guaranteed to please.

Heat the olive oil in a medium saucepan, add the onion and cook for 5 minutes, or until softened but not browned.

Stir the spice and curry powder into the onion, and then add the tomatoes and stock cube. Bring the sauce to the boil – stirring until the stock cube is dissolved. Reduce the heat, cover the pan and cook gently for 10–15 minutes.

Meanwhile, bring a large saucepan of lightly salted water to the boil, add the pasta and cook for 4–5 minutes, or as instructed on the packet, until soft.

Drain the cooked pasta and divide it between two warm pasta bowls or plates. Stir the capers into the sauce, pour over the pasta, sprinkle with the Parmesan cheese and serve immediately.

20

If preferred, use dried pasta instead of fresh. Cook according to the packet's instructions.

Time	15 minutes
Calories per portion	834 Kcal
Fat per portion	38g
of which saturated	11.3g
Serves	2
Suitable for vegetarians	

Penne pasta 200g (7oz)
Tender stem broccoli 250g (9oz)
Olive oil 3 tbsp, plus extra for serving
Salt and freshly ground black pepper
Garlic 2 cloves, peeled and thinly sliced
Red chilli 1, deseeded and finely sliced
Dried breadcrumbs 4 tbsp
Soft goat's cheese 150g (5oz), cut into chunks
Toasted pine nuts 2 tbsp

Goat's cheese and broccoli pasta

Sweet tenderstem broccoli contrasting with velvety goat's cheese – just gorgeous.

Bring a large saucepan of lightly salted water to the boil, add the pasta and cook as instructed on the packet or until al dente.

Meanwhile, toss the broccoli in 1 tablespoon of the olive oil and some seasoning. Heat a griddle pan until hot and add the broccoli and griddle for 6 minutes, until charred all over, then add a splash of water and cook for 1–2 minutes, or until tender.

Heat the remaining olive oil in a pan and fry the garlic and red chilli for 1 minute. Add the breadcrumbs and fry for a further 3 minutes, until golden and crisp.

Drain the pasta, add the broccoli and chilli breadcrumbs and toss together. Stir in the goat's cheese and toasted pine nuts, drizzle over a little olive oil and serve.

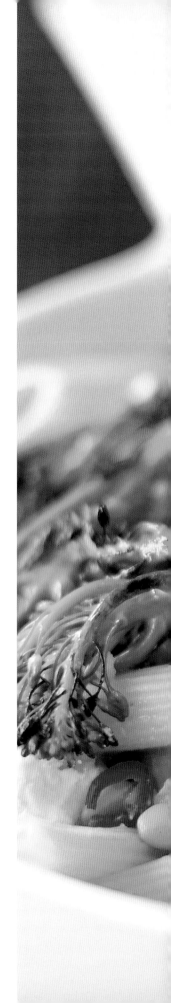

If you don't have a griddle pan, simply use a frying pan instead – the end result will be just as tasty.

Time	15 minutes
Calories per portion	763 Kcal
Fat per portion	40g
of which saturated	10.8g
Serves	2
Suitable for vegetarians if using a Parmesan substitute	

Pasta shapes 200g (7oz)
Marinated mixed mushrooms in oil
270g jar, drained
Walnut pieces 25g (1oz), roughly
chopped, plus extra for serving
Parmesan cheese 4 tbsp finely
grated, plus shavings for serving
Crème fraîche 2 tbsp
Salt and freshly ground black
pepper
Chopped flatleaf parsley 2 tbsp

15

Wild mushroom and walnut pasta

An unusual, yet flavoursome, vegetarian pasta dish.

Bring a large saucepan of lightly salted water to the boil, add the pasta and cook as instructed on the packet or until al dente. Drain well and return to the pan.

Meanwhile, put the marinated mushrooms in a bowl with the walnut pieces and mix with the Parmesan cheese and crème fraîche. Season and add the parsley. Toss through the pasta and heat gently for 1–2 minutes.

Serve piping hot with more walnut pieces and plenty of shaved Parmesan cheese.

If you can't find marinated mixed mushrooms, use wild mushrooms in oil instead.

Time	25 minutes
Calories per portion	122 Kcal
Fat per portion	6g
of which saturated	0.9g
Serves	2
Suitable for vegetarians	
Suitable for freezing	

Olive oil **1 tbsp**
Onion **1, peeled and chopped**
Large flat mushrooms **200g (7oz), wiped and thickly sliced**
Tomato purée **1 tbsp**
Red wine **100ml (3½fl oz)**
Vegetable stock **100ml (3½fl oz)**
Thyme leaves **a small handful**
Salt and freshly ground black pepper

Mushroom, red wine and thyme ragu

Rich and delicious – real comfort food.

Heat the olive oil in a wide saucepan over a medium heat. Add the onion and cook for 5 minutes until softened and then stir in the mushrooms. Cover and cook for 5 minutes, until the mushrooms have released some juice. Uncover and cook for a few more minutes to evaporate the juice.

Stir in the tomato purée. Cook for 30 seconds, then stir in the red wine and let it bubble for a few minutes to reduce by half. Stir in the vegetable stock with the thyme leaves. Again, let the ragú bubble for a few minutes until it has reduced a little, then season.

Serve with mashed potato, topped with more fresh thyme, and steamed broccoli.

Chestnut (or brown) mushrooms have a mild, nutty flavour and a firm meaty texture. They are perfect for baking as they retain their shape and texture well when cooked.

Time	25 minutes
Calories per portion	624 Kcal
Fat per portion	49g
of which saturated	16.9g
Serves	2
Suitable for vegetarians if using a Parmesan substitute	

Ready-rolled puff pastry 200g (7oz)
Green pesto sauce 2 tbsp
Chestnut mushrooms 12, wiped
Olive oil 1 tbsp
Parmesan cheese 25g (1oz), grated
Pine nuts 15g (½oz)
Freshly ground black pepper
Wild rocket a handful
Basil leaves a handful

Mushroom and pesto tarts

These savoury pastries are perfect for a snack or light supper when you don't want to compromise on flavour.

Preheat the oven to 220°C/Gas 7 and grease a large baking sheet.

Roll out the pastry on a floured surface to form a rectangle 25 x 13cm (10 x 5in). Cut in half to form two squares.

Arrange the pastry squares on the baking sheet and spread half the pesto sauce on each square to within 1cm (½in) of the edge.

Trim the mushroom stalks and then cut a thin slice off the top of each mushroom. Arrange six of them in the centre of each pastry square, stalks uppermost.

Drizzle with oil and sprinkle with Parmesan and the pine nuts. Season with black pepper. Bake in the oven for 15–18 minutes until the pastry is risen and golden, and the mushrooms are tender.

Serve warm, piled with rocket and basil leaves.

25

EVERYDAY EATING

Time	30 minutes
Calories per portion	554 Kcal
Fat per portion	32.9g
of which saturated	1.5g
Serves	2
Suitable for vegetarians	
Suitable for freezing	

Sliced bread 4 slices, crusts removed
Butter 25g (1oz)
Tomatoes 2, sliced
Mature Cheddar cheese 75g (3oz), grated
Eggs 2
Milk 150ml (¼ pint)
Salt and freshly ground black pepper

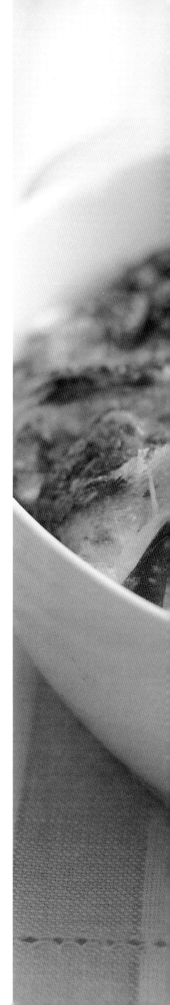

Cheese and tomato bake

This comforting combination is rather like eating a hot cheese and tomato sandwich.

Preheat the oven to 200°C/Gas 6 and place a baking sheet in the oven to heat up.

Cut the slices of bread in half diagonally, spread with butter on one side and arrange them, overlapping, in a small gratin dish. Insert the slices of tomato between the bread and then scatter over the cheese, lifting up some of the bread slices so that some cheese goes under the bread.

Use a fork to beat the eggs into the milk and season with salt and pepper. Pour the milk over the bread.

Place the dish on the heated baking sheet and bake in the centre of the oven for about 25 minutes, until the top is a light golden colour and it feels firm when lightly pressed in the centre. Remove from the oven and serve immediately.

This recipe is particularly good for
using up bread that has gone slightly
stale in the bread bin.

Buy only fresh fish for this dish, and make this recipe on the same day.

Time	30 minutes
Calories per portion	443 Kcal
Fat per portion	18.3g
of which saturated	0.9g
Serves	4

Teriyaki marinade **6 tbsp**
Lemon **½**, grated zest and **2 tbsp** juice
Chilli powder **¼ tsp**
Tuna, cod or halibut steaks **4 x 200g (7oz)**
New potatoes **400g (14oz)**, cut into thin slices, skins on
Butter **40g (1½oz)**
Button mushrooms **250g (9oz)**, wiped and sliced
Spring onions **6 large**, trimmed and sliced lengthways
Chopped coriander **4 tbsp**

Seared marinated fish steaks with mushrooms and potatoes

Teriyaki marinade, lemon and chilli powder ensure that this dish is full of Eastern promise.

Put the teriyaki marinade, lemon zest and juice and chilli powder into a wide, shallow dish. Add the fish steaks, turn them over in the marinade until evenly coated, then cover and set aside.

Gently steam the potatoes for 20 minutes, or until cooked, but not broken up.

Meanwhile, melt half of the butter in a large frying pan, add the mushrooms and cook gently for 3–4 minutes, until softened and lightly browned, then remove from the pan and keep hot.

Wipe the pan clean with kitchen paper, then add and melt the remaining butter. Transfer the fish steaks and marinade to the frying pan and cook for 2–3 minutes on each side until the fish is cooked through, but taking care not to overcook. Transfer onto warmed plates and keep warm.

Add the spring onions to the pan juices and cook for 3–4 minutes until softened. Mix in the potatoes, mushrooms and coriander and serve alongside the tuna steaks.

In place of haddock, try tilapia, which is equally fleshy and tasty.

Time	15 minutes
Calories per portion	286 Kcal
Fat per portion	14g
of which saturated	6.4g
Serves	2

Olive oil for oiling the baking sheet
and drizzling
Haddock fillets 2 x 150g (5oz),
skinned
Salt and freshly ground black
pepper
Tomato 1, thinly sliced
Emmental 60g (2½oz), grated
Wholegrain mustard 1 tsp
Snipped chives 2 tbsp

Haddock cheese melts

Super-quick and delicately delicious.

Preheat the grill to medium-hot. Line a baking sheet with baking paper and lightly brush with olive oil. Lay the haddock fillets on the paper and season.

Arrange the tomato on top of the fish pieces, slightly overlapping, and lightly drizzle with oil. Grill for 2–3 minutes.

Meanwhile, mix together the grated Emmental, wholegrain mustard and chives. Remove the fish from the grill and pile the cheese mixture on top of the tomatoes. Return to the grill and cook for a further 6–7 minutes, until the cheese is bubbling and the fish is just cooked through.

Season and serve with a crisp green salad.

Time	20 minutes
Calories per portion	261 Kcal
Fat per portion	14g
of which saturated	7.1g
Serves	2

Lemon 1, finely grated zest, plus 2 tsp juice
Sea bass fillets 2 x 110g (4oz)
Ciabatta bread 25g (1oz), torn into crumbs
Spring onions 2, trimmed and finely sliced
Chopped parsley 2 tbsp
Salt and freshly ground black pepper
Butter 25g (1oz), melted

Crusted sea bass

The crunchy herby topping in this recipe contrasts with the delicate white flesh of the fish.

Preheat the oven to 200°C/Gas 6. Brush the lemon juice over the flesh of the fish fillets and place the fillets, skin side down, on a baking tray.

Tip the breadcrumbs into a bowl and stir in the lemon zest, spring onions, parsley and seasoning, and then stir in the butter. Press the crumb mixture on top of the fish fillets.

Bake the fish in the centre of the oven for 12–15 minutes, or until the crust is light golden in colour. Remove from the oven and serve immediately while it is piping hot.

Ready-made breadcrumbs save you time, but if you do make your own, then let them dry out a little before you use them.

Time	30 minutes
Calories per portion	281 Kcal
Fat per portion	14.9g
of which saturated	2.6g
Serves	4

Red chilli 1, deseeded and finely chopped
Caster sugar 2 tsp
Thai fish sauce 1 tsp
Lime juice 1 tbsp
Rice vinegar 1 tbsp
Cucumber ½, halved and cut into long, thin strips
Yellow pepper 1 small, deseeded and cut into long, thin strips
Carrot 1 small, peeled and cut into thin strips
Cherry tomatoes 12, halved
Skinned salmon fillets 500g (1lb 2oz)
Root ginger 4cm (1¾oz) piece, peeled and very finely chopped
Spring onions 4, trimmed and finely chopped
Salt and freshly ground black pepper
Vegetable oil 1 tsp
Coriander a bunch, stalks removed

Salmon and ginger fishcakes with sweet-and-sour salad

Thai inspired flavours without fuss.

For the salad, put the chilli, sugar, fish sauce, lime juice and vinegar into a screw-top jar and shake well. Set aside. Toss the cucumber, pepper, carrot and tomatoes together in a bowl.

Chop the salmon until you have a coarse, mince-like mixture. Put into another bowl with the ginger and spring onions and season to taste. Mix together and divide into eight. Using slightly wet hands, shape into eight fishcakes.

Heat the oil in a large, non-stick frying pan over a medium heat. Cook the fishcakes for 1½ minutes on each side, until lightly golden and cooked.

Toss the dressing and coriander leaves through the salad. Divide between four plates and top each with two fishcakes.

Chopping and preparation is so much easier with good equipment. Buy good-quality knives and always keep them sharp.

If you can't get rice wine vinegar, use the same amount of white wine vinegar mixed with a little caster sugar to sweeten it.

Time	15 minutes
Calories per portion	289 Kcal
Fat per portion	7.5g
of which saturated	1.5g
Serves	4

Sesame seeds 15g (½oz)
French beans 200g (7oz), topped and tailed and cut in half lengthways
Mangetout 200g (7oz), cut in half lengthways
Dried medium egg noodles 125g (4½oz)
Cooked and peeled prawns 400g (14oz)
Red chilli 1, deseeded and chopped

For the dressing
Dark soy sauce 1 tbsp
Rice wine vinegar 1 tbsp
Toasted sesame oil 1 tsp
Vegetable oil 1 tsp
Caster sugar ¼ tsp

French bean, prawn and sesame noodles

The crunch of seeds and mangetout contrasts with the spicy, succulent noodles.

Heat a dry frying pan over a medium-high heat. Add the sesame seeds and stir for 3–4 minutes, until lightly toasted. Transfer the seeds to a bowl and leave them to cool. Whisk together the ingredients for the dressing.

Meanwhile, bring a large pan of salted water to the boil. Drop the beans into the pan and cook for 3 minutes, until just tender. Remove with a slotted spoon and refresh under cold water. Add the mangetout and cook for 2 minutes. Remove with a slotted spoon, then drain and refresh as before.

Add the noodles to the pan and cook for 4 minutes or until just al dente. Drain and set aside to cool.

Mix together the beans, mangetout, noodles, prawns, most of the sesame seeds and the chilli in a large bowl. Add the dressing and toss together well. Sprinkle with the rest of the sesame seeds just before serving.

Time	15 minutes
Calories per portion	510 Kcal
Fat per portion	15g
of which saturated	5.2g
Serves	2

Frozen pea and bean mix 150g (5oz)
Pasta shapes 150g (5oz)
Vegetable oil 1 tbsp
Shallots 3, peeled and diced
Chives small bunch, snipped
Crème fraîche 2 tbsp
Lemons 2, zest and juice of 1, the other cut into wedges
White crab meat 200g (7oz) fresh or canned, shredded

Crab and lemon farfalle

Tangy lemon-infused pasta mixed with greens and tasty crab meat.

Bring a small pan of salted water to the boil and cook the frozen peas and beans for 3 minutes, then drain and refresh in cold water. Remove the broad beans from their skins if you like, and set aside.

Meanwhile, bring a saucepan of lightly salted water to the boil, add the pasta and cook as instructed on the packet or until al dente.

At the same time, heat the vegetable oil in a frying pan and sweat the shallots for 5 minutes until softened.

Drain the pasta and add the chives along with the beans, peas and softened shallots. Stir through the crème fraîche, lemon zest and juice and the crab meat.

Divide between shallow bowls and serve with the lemon wedges to squeeze over.

To prevent pasta from sticking together, add 1 teaspoon olive oil to the water with the pasta.

For a professional finish, cut the cooked chicken breasts on the diagonal into thick slices. Garnish with a handful of wild rocket drizzled with balsamic vinegar and olive oil.

Time	30 minutes
Calories per portion	612 Kcal
Fat per portion	37g
of which saturated	16.3g
Serves	2

Skinless chicken breasts 2
Boursin cheese with garlic and herbs 100g (3½oz)
Prosciutto 4 slices
Olive oil 2 tbsp
Salt and freshly ground black pepper
Green lentils 410g can, rinsed and drained
Spring onions 3, trimmed and finely chopped
Mild red chilli 1, deseeded and chopped
Lime 1, juice only
Chopped coriander 3 tbsp

Prosciutto-wrapped chicken breasts on a bed of green lentils

Classic stuffed chicken served with spiced lentils.

Preheat the oven to 200°C/Gas 6.

Make a slit horizontally in each chicken breast. Divide the cheese into two portions, roll slightly and use to stuff the slit in the chicken.

Carefully wrap each chicken breast with two slices of prosciutto so the cheese is totally encased. Pop the wrapped chicken in a roasting tin, sprinkle with 1 tablespoon of the olive oil, season with freshly ground black pepper and roast for 20–25 minutes, or until the chicken is cooked through.

Meanwhile, pop the lentils, spring onions, chilli and remaining oil in a pan. Heat gently, stirring all the time, for 4–5 minutes until piping hot, but do not boil or it will impair the flavour. Remove the pan from the heat and season with lime juice, coriander and salt.

Cut the chicken breasts into slices (see opposite). Arrange the lentils on serving plates and set the chicken breasts on top.

Time	25 minutes
Calories per portion	363 Kcal
Fat per portion	7g
of which saturated	2.5g
Serves	2

Stem ginger in syrup 3 globes, drained and finely diced
Runny honey 2 tbsp
Soy sauce 2 tbsp
Limes 2, finely grated zest of both, juice of 1
Garlic 2 cloves, peeled and crushed
Skinless chicken thighs 6

Sticky lime and ginger chicken

Sweet, yet savoury succulent chicken pieces, baked to perfection.

Preheat the oven to 230°C/Gas 8.

Mix the ginger with the honey, soy sauce, lime zest and juice and garlic in a bowl. Add the chicken thighs and mix together well.

Spread out the prepared chicken in a foil-lined or ceramic baking dish and bake in the oven for 20 minutes, turning over halfway, until cooked through.

Serve the chicken together with steamed basmati rice and some tender stem broccoli.

The chicken could also be served shredded on a bed of noodles, sprinkled with sesame oil.

To make vinaigrette, whisk 2 teaspoons Dijon mustard with 2 tablespoons white wine vinegar and 6 tablespoons olive oil.

Time	30 minutes
Calories per portion	494 Kcal
Fat per portion	28g
of which saturated	8.8g
Serves	2

Olive oil for oiling a baking tray and to drizzle
Skinless chicken breasts 2
Salt and freshly ground black pepper
Mozzarella 4 slices
Ready-roasted peppers 4 from a jar
Basil leaves a few
Vine-ripened cherry tomatoes a handful
Baby spinach leaves a handful
Toasted pine nuts 1 tbsp
Ready-made croutons a handful
Vinaigrette to serve

Stuffed Mediterranean chicken with spinach salad and roast tomatoes

Healthy, wholesome Italian food at its best.

Preheat the oven to 220°C/Gas 7 and lightly oil a baking tray.

Make slits along the sides of the chicken breasts to make a large pocket in each. Season inside and out. Stuff each generously with 2 slices of mozzarella, a couple of ready-roasted peppers and some basil leaves.

Place on the baking tray with the tomatoes and drizzle with a little more olive oil. Roast for 20 minutes until the chicken is cooked through and the tomatoes are soft.

Meanwhile, toss the spinach with the pine nuts and croutons. Dress the salad with the vinaigrette and serve alongside the chicken and roasted tomatoes.

Time	30 minutes
Calories per portion	805 Kcal
Fat per portion	57g
of which saturated	27.4g
Serves	2
Suitable for freezing	

Vegetable oil 1 tbsp
Garlic 1 large clove, peeled and finely chopped
Spring onions 1 bunch, trimmed and thinly sliced
Sweetcorn 250g (9oz)
Parmesan cheese 25g (1oz), grated
Double cream 150ml (¼ pint)
White wine 75ml (2½fl oz)
Salt and freshly ground black pepper
Skinless chicken breasts 2
Smoked streaky bacon 2 rashers

Chicken and creamy sweetcorn bake

Warming, simple food – hassle-free.

Preheat the oven to 220°C/Gas 7.

In a frying pan, heat the oil and gently fry the garlic and spring onions for about 2 minutes, until softened.

Mix the garlic and spring onions with the sweetcorn, Parmesan cheese, double cream and white wine in a large bowl. Season well and transfer into a medium ovenproof dish.

Season the chicken breasts and place on top of the sweetcorn. Then arrange a bacon rasher over each breast and cook in the oven for 25 minutes, or until the chicken is cooked through and the bacon is crispy.

Replace the white wine with
an equal quantity of chicken
stock if you prefer.

71

For a vegetarian option, replace the meat with 1 diced courgette and 400g (14oz) diced and marinated haloumi. Grill for 2 minutes per side.

Time	30 minutes
Calories per portion	533 Kcal
Fat per portion	28.5g
of which saturated	8.2g
Serves	4

Skinless chicken breasts 2 large
Smoked hot paprika ½ tsp
Garlic 1 clove, peeled and crushed
Lemon 1, grated zest and juice
Olive oil 1 tbsp
Salt and freshly ground black pepper
Roasted red peppers in oil 280g jar
Small onion 1, peeled and thinly sliced
Chorizo 75g (3oz) piece, skinned and diced
Warmed tortilla wraps 8
Soured cream 142ml pot, to serve
Mixed leaves to serve

Chicken and chorizo wraps

Hearty wraps full of flavour and colour.

Cut the chicken into large chunks and put in a mixing bowl with the paprika, garlic, lemon zest and juice and oil. Season, toss together and marinate for 15 minutes.

Meanwhile, make the sauce. Drain and roughly chop the peppers, reserving 2 tablespoons of the oil. Heat the reserved oil in a large frying pan over a medium heat. Add the onion and cook, stirring, for 5 minutes, until softened. Then add the peppers, chorizo and a splash of water. Cover and simmer over a low heat for 5 minutes, until the sauce is thickened. Season to taste and then re-cover the pan and keep warm.

Preheat the grill to medium-hot. Thread the marinated chicken onto metal or wooden skewers (if using wooden skewers, soak them first in water to prevent scorching). Grill for about 5 minutes each side, until the chicken is cooked through.

Remove the chicken from the skewers and serve in the wraps with the sauce, soured cream and mixed dressed salad.

Time	25 minutes
Calories per portion	870 Kcal
Fat per portion	54g
of which saturated	29.9g
Serves	2

Potatoes 300g (11oz), peeled and cut into even-sized pieces
Butter 15g (½oz), plus extra for the mashed potato
Sweetcorn 198g can, drained
Plain flour 2 tbsp
Chilli powder 1 tsp
Skinless chicken breasts 2
White wine a splash
Double cream 150ml (¼ pint)
Salt and freshly ground black pepper
Flat leaf parsley to serve

Southern-fried chicken with corn mash

Perfectly spiced chicken served with flavoured mash and a creamy sauce.

Cook the potatoes in boiling salted water for 12 minutes, until tender. Drain and mash with a knob of butter and the sweetcorn. Keep warm.

Meanwhile, mix the plain flour with the chilli powder on a large plate and then toss the chicken breasts in the chilli flour, shaking off any excess.

Melt the 15g (½oz) of butter in a frying pan and cook the chicken for 5–6 minutes on each side until golden and tender (be careful not to let the butter burn). Push the chicken to one side and then add a splash of white wine to the pan. Let it bubble for 1 minute, then add the double cream, bring to the boil and cook briefly until just thickened. Season well.

Spoon the sweetcorn mash onto plates, add the chicken and pour over the sauce. Scatter with parsley to serve.

25

For a touch of variety, omit the sweetcorn and add a handful of chopped herbs to the mash.

Time	25 minutes
Calories per portion	901 Kcal
Fat per portion	61.3g
of which saturated	2.3g
Serves	2
Suitable for freezing	

Ready-roasted chicken breasts 2
Olive oil 1 tbsp
Butter a knob
Baby leeks 110g (4oz), trimmed and
thickly sliced
Smoked bacon lardons 75g (3oz)
Mustard and tarragon or honey
cooking sauce 175g (6oz)
Double cream 90ml (3fl oz)
Salt and freshly ground black
pepper
Ready-made mashed potato with
cheese 450g pack

Chicken and leek pot pies

Mmmm, warm and comforting – and fast, too.

Preheat the grill to high. Remove the skin from the ready-roasted chicken breasts, and thickly slice the meat.

In a sauté pan, heat the olive oil and a knob of butter, then fry the baby leeks and smoked bacon lardons for 3 minutes.

Add the chicken and cook for 2 minutes more. Pour over the mustard and tarragon cooking sauce and double cream and add a splash of water into the pan. Let it gently bubble until warmed through, check the seasoning and then spoon between two 500ml (18fl oz) pie dishes.

Meanwhile, cook the ready-made mashed potato with cheese in the microwave according to the pack's instructions and turn on the grill to high. Spoon the mash over the pies and pop them under the grill for 3 minutes to brown.

25

Take care when adding salt to this recipe as the lardons and cooking sauce are salty already.

Any leftovers make a great sandwich filling with a bit of garlic mayonnaise.

Time	30 minutes
Calories per portion	351 Kcal
Fat per portion	19g
of which saturated	5.9g
Serves	4

Saffron threads **a pinch**
Boiling water **1 tbsp**
Skinless chicken breasts **4**
Plain flour **1 tbsp**
Egg **1, beaten**
Freshly ground black pepper
Olive oil **4 tbsp**
Finely grated Grana Padano cheese
8 tbsp
Chopped thyme **1 tbsp, plus extra
sprigs to garnish**
Lemon wedges **to serve**

Pan-fried chicken in a Grana Padano crust

Cooking chicken breasts quickly and in a crust like this guarantees they stay juicy and succulent.

Put the saffron in a bowl, add the boiling water and set aside for a few minutes to infuse.

Meanwhile, cut the chicken in half widthways to make 8 thin pieces and dust very lightly in flour.

Crack the egg into the bowl of saffron. Add a good grinding of black pepper and beat well.

Heat half the oil in a large frying pan over a medium heat. Mix together the cheese and thyme on a plate. Dip the chicken first in the egg mixture, then coat in the Grana Padano mixture.

Fry in two batches, adding the remaining oil with the second batch, until crisp, golden and cooked through. It should take about 5 minutes on each side, but don't be tempted to lift or turn the chicken too soon or the crust might stick to the bottom of the pan.

Serve with herb mash and lemon wedges to squeeze over. Garnish with thyme.

If you want to prepare in advance for a barbeque, simply wrap the burgers in cling film and store in the fridge.

Time	25 minutes
Calories per portion	331 Kcal
Fat per portion	6.5g
of which saturated	1.5g
Serves	4
Burgers are suitable for freezing	

For the burgers
Turkey mince 500g (1lb 2oz)
Garlic 2 large cloves, peeled and crushed
Ground cumin 1 tsp
Tomato purée 1 tbsp
Tabasco sauce ½–1 tsp, to taste
Lime 1, grated zest
Onion 1 small, peeled and grated
Salt and freshly ground black pepper
Olive oil for brushing
Beef tomato 1, thickly sliced
Little gem lettuce leaves 8
Ciabatta rolls 4

For the watercress tzatziki
0% fat natural yogurt 200g tub
Garlic 1 large clove, peeled and crushed
Lime juice 1 tbsp
Watercress 40g (2½oz), finely chopped
Dried mint 1 tbsp

Harissa turkey burgers with a watercress tzatziki

A tangy twist on standard burgers – just right!

Preheat the barbecue or grill to medium.

To make the tzatziki, mix together all the ingredients in a bowl. Season to taste.

For the burgers, mix together the turkey mince, garlic, cumin, tomato purée, Tabasco, lime zest and onion in a bowl with your hands. Season well.

Divide into four and form into burgers. Brush the burgers with a little oil and barbecue or grill for 15 minutes, until cooked, turning halfway. Split the rolls in half and barbecue or grill until toasted.

To serve, put the tomato and lettuce in the ciabatta rolls and top each with a burger and some tzatziki.

25

EVERYDAY EATING

Half-fat crème fraîche is readily available if you want to keep the calories down.

Time	20 minutes
Calories per portion	634 Kcal
Fat per portion	47g
of which saturated	24.2g
Serves	4

Butter a knob for cooking
Salt and freshly ground black pepper
Pork chops or loin steaks 4
Ready-to-eat prunes 200g (7oz), stoned and halved
White wine a good splash (optional)
Crème fraîche 200ml tub

Pork chops with prunes in crème fraîche

Sweet soft prunes provide the perfect accompaniment to salty pork chops.

Add the knob of butter to a large frying pan over a high heat and season the pork chops. When hot, add the chops and cook for 2–3 minutes on each side to brown all over.

Add the prunes and white wine, if using. Boil to reduce by half, then stir in the crème fraîche. Simmer for 2–3 minutes, or until the pork is cooked through and the sauce thickened.

Check the seasoning and divide between four plates. The chops are delicious served with steamed curly kale and mash.

Time	25 minutes
Calories per portion	512 Kcal
Fat per portion	27g
of which saturated	10.3g
Serves	4

Pork and herb sausages 6, cut into large chunks
Chestnut mushrooms 250g (9oz), wiped and thickly sliced
Chopped tomatoes 400g can
Flat leaf parsley a handful
Salt and freshly ground black pepper
Quick-cook polenta 200g (7oz)
Mature Cheddar cheese 75g (3oz), finely grated

Sausage ragu on cheesy polenta

Sausage and mash with the flavour of Italy.

Heat a frying pan over a medium-high heat – there's no need to add any oil. When hot, add the sausages and cook, stirring, for 3–4 minutes, until browned.

Add the mushrooms and cook for a few minutes, stirring, to soften. Then add the chopped tomatoes and simmer for 10 minutes, until reduced and thickened slightly. Tear over half of the parsley leaves and season to taste.

Meanwhile, bring 1 litre (1¾ pints) of water to the boil in a large saucepan over a high heat. Reduce the heat to low, whisk in the polenta and cook, stirring continuously, for 1 minute, or as directed on the pack, until really thick.

Remove the polenta from the heat and stir in the Cheddar until it has melted. Season with salt and pepper to taste and divide between four plates. Spoon over the sausage ragu and scatter with the remaining parsley leaves to serve.

25:

Try using a different variety of sausage, such as sweet chilli, and add a finely chopped chilli to the polenta for some spicy kick.

Time	25 minutes
Calories per portion	778 Kcal
Fat per portion	33g
of which saturated	9.6g
Serves	2

Fresh ricotta and spinach ravioli or tortellini 250g pack
Marinated and grilled/roasted peppers 50g (2oz), drained and
chopped into large chunks
Red and yellow cherry tomatoes 8, halved
Chorizo 6 thin slices
Tomato pasta sauce 250g pot
Mozzarella ½ x 125g ball, cut into slices
Garlic and herb bread ½ x 270g loaf
Basil leaves to serve

Ravioli pasta bake

*Sweet, slightly spicy pasta with a wonderfully original
crusty topping.*

Preheat the oven to 200°C/Gas 6.

Tip the ravioli or tortellini into a 1.25 litre (2 pint) ovenproof dish.
Mix with the peppers, cherry tomatoes,and chorizo slices. Stir
through the tomato pasta sauce, thinned down with 100ml (3½fl oz)
water, and scatter with the mozzarella.

Bake in the oven for 10 minutes, then crumble over the garlic and
herb bread and return to the oven for another 10 minutes, until
golden and cooked through. Scatter with a few basil leaves to serve.

*Use up the leftover
mozzarella with basil
leaves, tomatoes and
avocado and serve with
the remaining garlic and
herb bread.*

If you don't have fresh tagliatelle to hand, replace it with dried pasta from your storecupboard.

82

Time	15 minutes
Calories per portion	713 Kcal
Fat per portion	40g
of which saturated	21.1g
Serves	4

Streaky bacon **12 rashers**
Courgettes **2 large, trimmed and coarsely grated**
Lemon **1, finely grated zest**
Crème fraîche **250ml tub**
Salt and freshly ground black pepper
Fresh tagliatelle **500g pack**
Parmesan shavings **to garnish (optional)**

Pasta with courgettes and bacon

A light but delightful pasta dish that's ready in minutes.

Put a large saucepan of water on to boil, ready for the pasta. Dry-fry the bacon in a large, hot frying pan over a high heat for 5 minutes, turning halfway, until golden and crispy. Set aside on kitchen paper to cool, then roughly chop.

Reduce the heat slightly and add the courgettes to the frying pan. Cook for a few minutes, stirring, until just wilted. Stir in the lemon zest and crème fraîche and simmer for a few minutes – it will look quite runny. Season to taste and keep over a low heat.

Meanwhile, add the pack of tagliatelle to the saucepan of boiling water and cook for 2 minutes, until al dente. Drain well, return to the pan and add the courgette mixture. Toss well until the pasta has soaked up the sauce, then stir in the bacon.

Divide between shallow bowls and scatter with the Parmesan shavings, if you like.

EVERYDAY EATING

Time	15 minutes
Calories per portion	528 Kcal
Fat per portion	16g
of which saturated	5.4g
Serves	4

Rigatoni pasta 400g (14oz)
Streaky bacon 8 rashers, chopped
Red chilli 1 large, deseeded and chopped
Capers 2 tbsp, rinsed
Black olives 10, pitted and halved
Tomato pasta sauce 350g tub
Crème fraîche 2 tbsp
Salt and freshly ground black pepper

Crispy bacon, chilli and tomato rigatoni

A piquant and satisfying pasta supper.

Bring a large saucepan of lightly salted water to the boil, add the pasta and cook as instructed on the packet or until al dente.

Meanwhile, fry the bacon in a large frying pan for 5 minutes. Add the chilli and cook for 1 minute. Then add the capers, olives and tomato pasta sauce and warm through. When the pasta is cooked, drain it and transfer to a large serving bowl.

Stir the crème fraîche and bacon, chilli and tomato mixture into the pasta, season and serve.

To make this dish even more quickly, use fresh pasta rather than the dried version specified in the ingredients.

Time	30 minutes
Calories per portion	667 Kcal
Fat per portion	41.8g
of which saturated	7.9g
Serves	4

Lamb mince 500g (1lb 2oz) pack
Onion 1, peeled and finely chopped
Garlic 2 cloves, peeled and finely chopped
Red peppers 2, deseeded and diced
Red pesto sauce 190g jar
Chopped tomatoes 400g can
Pasta shapes 150g (5oz)

Red pesto lamb with pasta

Here is a tangy, tasty alternative to Bolognaise.

Heat a deep, wide frying pan over a medium heat. Add the mince, onion and garlic and fry for 5 minutes. Stir in the peppers, pesto and tomatoes and simmer for 20 minutes, stirring occasionally.

Meanwhile, bring a saucepan of lightly salted water to the boil, add the pasta and cook as instructed on the packet or until al dente.

Mix the pasta into the meat sauce and serve.

If you are really hungry, serve with a French stick spread with garlic butter and grated Caerphilly and baked in the oven.

Try using other dried fruit instead of the apricots, such as prunes or raisins.

25

EVERYDAY EATING

Time	25 minutes
Calories per portion	490 Kcal
Fat per portion	34g
of which saturated	12.5g
Serves	2
Suitable for freezing	

Lamb neck fillets 250g (9oz), cut into chunks
Onion 1 small, peeled and chopped
Ground allspice 1 tsp
Vegetable oil 2 tbsp
Salt and freshly ground black pepper
Chopped tomatoes 200g can
Chicken stock 150ml (¼ pint)
Ready-to-eat dried apricots 75g (3oz)
Couscous 150g (6oz)
Toasted flaked almonds to serve
Lemon wedges to serve

Spiced lamb with apricots and couscous

Moroccan lamb with sweet apricots and flaked almonds, designed to tickle those tastebuds.

Put the lamb fillets into a bowl and add the onion, ground allspice and vegetable oil. Season and mix together.

Heat a large frying pan. When hot, add the lamb mixture and cook for 5 minutes to brown the meat and soften the onion. Stir in the tomatoes, chicken stock and apricots and bring to the boil. Reduce the heat and simmer for 10 minutes until the lamb is cooked through and the sauce has thickened.

Cook the couscous as on the packet's instructions and divide between two warmed plates.

Season the lamb to taste, spoon over the couscous and scatter each portion with toasted flaked almonds. Serve with lemon wedges.

For the best result and flavour, buy
lean leg of lamb steaks and chop them
very finely (using two large knives),
or in a food processor. Bought, ready
minced lamb can lack flavour.

88

Time	20 minutes
Calories per portion	556 Kcal
Fat per portion	23g
of which saturated	8.1g
Serves	4
Suitable for freezing	

Lean minced lamb 400g (14oz)
Onion 1 small, peeled and very finely chopped
Ready-to-eat dried figs 150g (5oz), roughly chopped
Medium curry powder 1 tsp
Mixed spice 1 tsp
Chopped coriander 3 tbsp
Salt and freshly ground black pepper
Olive oil 2–3 tbsp
Large rolls or baps 4
Lettuce leaves such as Frisée or Curly Endive
Coriander a few sprigs

Lamb burgers with figs

Gourmet lamb burgers with style!

Put the minced lamb, onion, figs, curry powder, mixed spice and coriander into a mixing bowl. Add a little salt and pepper and mix together with your hand.

Divide the lamb mixture into four equal pieces and then shape each one, on a lightly floured board, into burgers about 2.5cm (1in) thick.

Heat the olive oil in a frying pan, then add the burgers and cook for 5–6 minutes. Carefully turn them over and cook the other side for another 5–6 minutes until golden brown, and the burgers are cooked through.

To serve, put each burger in a roll or bap together with some lettuce leaves and coriander sprigs.

Experiment with different curry pastes. Thai green works well, as does balti.

Time	15 minutes
Calories per portion	1162 Kcal
Fat per portion	59g
of which saturated	39g
Serves	2

Coconut milk 400ml can
Curry paste 2 tbsp
Basmati rice 150g (5oz), rinsed
Frozen broad beans 200g (7oz)
Lamb leg steaks 4
Mint leaves to garnish

Spicy lamb steaks with coconut and broad bean rice

These lamb steaks rest comfortably on a bed of delicately flavoured rice.

Pour the coconut milk into a saucepan and stir in 1½ tablespoons of the curry paste. Then add the rice and cook gently, uncovered, for 12 minutes or until just tender. The rice will absorb most of the coconut milk, leaving you with a lovely risotto-like mixture.

Meanwhile, cook the broad beans in boiling salted water for 2–3 minutes, until tender. Drain and stir into the rice.

Brush the lamb steaks with the remaining curry paste and grill for 4–5 minutes on each side until tender. Divide the rice between plates and top with the lamb. Garnish with mint leaves before serving.

Time	15 minutes
Calories per portion	736 Kcal
Fat per portion	34g
of which saturated	9.3g
Serves	2
Suitable for freezing	

Beef mince 250g (9oz)
Onion 1 small, peeled and chopped
Baked beans in tomato sauce 415g
can
Worcestershire sauce 2 tbsp
Dried mixed herbs 1 tbsp
Salt and freshly ground black
pepper
Chilled flavoured mashed potato
450g pack

Quick cottage pie

The perfect comfort food in an unbelievable time!

Heat a large, dry frying pan over a high heat. Add the beef mince and onion and cook, stirring to break up the meat, for 3–4 minutes, until the meat is browned.

Stir in the baked beans, Worcestershire sauce, dried mixed herbs, some seasoning and a good dash of water. Simmer rapidly for 3–4 minutes, until thickened and then tip the pie filling into a deep 1.25 litre (2 pint) baking dish.

Meanwhile, preheat the grill to hot. Heat the mashed potato according to the pack instructions, spoon on top of the mince and rough up the surface. Pop under the hot grill for a few minutes, until golden and bubbling.

15

Supermarkets sell flavoured mash, such as colcannon, in the chilled food section. Use plain mash, if you prefer.

Time	15 minutes
Calories per portion	483 Kcal
Fat per portion	23g
of which saturated	14.1g
Serves	3

Beef and red wine tortelloni or other stuffed pasta 250-300g pack
Parmesan cheese 65g (2½oz), finely grated
Mascarpone 250g tub
Freshly ground black pepper
Chopped tomatoes 400g can
Basil leaves a handful, plus extra to garnish

Cheat's lasagne

Creamy, indulgent, delicious – and so speedy!

Preheat the grill to hot. Cook the stuffed pasta in a saucepan of boiling water for 3 minutes. Drain it well and then tip into a wide ovenproof dish.

Meanwhile, mix 25g (1oz) of the Parmesan with the mascarpone and season with black pepper.

Pour the chopped tomatoes over the pasta, tear over most of the basil leaves and gently toss together. Then dot over the mascarpone mixture and scatter with the remaining Parmesan.

Pop under the hot grill for 3–4 minutes, until bubbling and golden. Garnish with fresh basil leaves.

This is very rich, so it only needs a simple side salad, such as mixed green leaves dressed with a sprinkle of balsamic vinegar.

Time	20 minutes
Calories per portion	581 Kcal
Fat per portion	26.6g
of which saturated	12.9g
Serves	4

Long grain rice 225g (8oz)
Quick-frying/minute beef steaks
500g (1lb 2oz), cut into thin strips
Mixed peppercorns 1 tsp, crushed
Olive oil 1 tbsp
Onion 1, peeled and finely sliced
Closed cup mushrooms 150g (5oz),
wiped and halved
Soured cream 284ml carton
Paprika 2 tsp

20

Speedy beef stroganoff

A really easy – yet still tasty – version of a true classic.

Bring a pan of lightly salted water to the boil and add the rice. Turn down the heat, cover and leave to simmer for 10 minutes, until the rice is just cooked. Rinse in a sieve with boiling water.

Meanwhile, put the beef strips into a shallow dish, add the crushed peppercorns and toss to coat. Set aside.

Heat the olive oil in a large frying pan over a medium heat and cook the onion for 3–4 minutes or until soft but not coloured. Add the mushrooms and cook for a further 5 minutes.

Increase the heat, add the beef strips and fry for 4–5 minutes or until the juices have evaporated and the meat is brown. Add 3 tablespoons of water and let it bubble to deglaze the pan.

Stir in most of the soured cream and half the paprika, and gently heat until warmed through. Check the seasoning.

Spoon the beef stroganoff onto plates. Top with the remaining soured cream. Season with the remaining paprika and some more black pepper and serve with the rice.

For a lower fat version, use some low fat crème fraîche in place of the soured cream.

Serve with oven chips or home-made potato wedges (see page 127).

Time	10 minutes
Calories per portion	660 Kcal
Fat per portion	50g
of which saturated	15.7g
Serves	2

Sirloin steaks 2
Olive oil for brushing
Salt and freshly ground black pepper
Garlic 1 clove, peeled and crushed
Tarragon a small handful, chopped
Mayonnaise 4 tbsp
Caramelised onion chutney (or similar) 2 large tbsp
Blue cheese 2 thin slices

Grilled steaks with caramelised onions and garlic mayo

Perfect pub grub from the comfort of your own home.

Heat a griddle pan until very hot. Brush the steaks lightly with some olive oil, then season and char grill for 2–3 minutes on each side, depending on how you like your steaks.

Meanwhile, make the garlic mayonnaise by stirring the garlic and tarragon into the mayonnaise. Set aside.

Preheat the grill to hot. Put a dollop of chutney on each steak and top each with a slice of blue cheese and then pop under the grill for 2 minutes. Serve with the garlic mayonnaise.

Be sure to buy only lean meat to ensure you get the right weight.

Time	15 minutes
Calories per portion	674 Kcal
Fat per portion	40.1g
of which saturated	1.8g
Serves	2

Trimmed rump steaks 225–275g (8–10oz)
Olive oil 1 tbsp
Salt and freshly ground black pepper
Soured cream 3 tbsp
Mayonnaise 3 tbsp
Celery 2 sticks, thinly sliced
Crisp lettuce leaves roughly torn into pieces
Pitted, tenderised prunes 40g (1½oz), roughly chopped
Sun-dried tomatoes in olive oil 40g (1½oz), drained and roughly chopped
Large cooked and peeled king or tiger prawns 12, thawed and well drained if frozen

Surf and turf salad

A fresh and fruity dish, that is packed with flavour.

Wipe the rump steaks with clean kitchen paper, then put them onto a plate, brush both sides with olive oil and season well with salt and pepper. Cover and set aside while preparing the salad.

Put the soured cream and mayonnaise into a salad bowl and mix well. Add the celery, lettuce leaves, prunes and sun-dried tomatoes and then set aside while cooking the steaks.

Heat a large frying pan or ridged grill pan until hot. Add the steak and cook for 4–5 minutes on each side, yet still slightly pink in the middle, or cooked to your preference. Remove from the pan and cut into thin slices.

Add the beef and prawns to the salad, toss gently together and serve immediately.

Frozen assets

Freeze your 'frozen asset' in advance - the perfect base for two deliciously different creations.

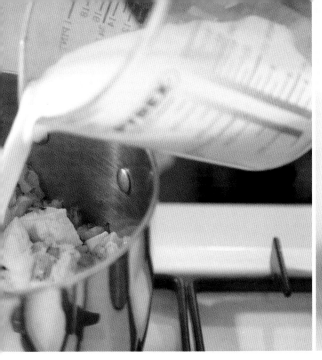

Time	10 minutes plus standing time
Makes	2 bases
Suitable for vegetarians, depending on the topping	
Suitable for freezing	

Strong plain flour 450g (1lb)
Quick yeast 1 level tsp
Caster sugar 1 level tsp
Salt 1 tsp
Olive oil 1 tbsp
Warm water 300ml (½ pint)

Pizza bases

Homemade pizzas are just simply the best!

Sift the flour, yeast, sugar and salt into a mixing bowl, make a well in the centre and add the olive oil. Gradually adding the water, mix well together until you have a soft dough. Then turn out onto a lightly floured work surface and knead for 5 minutes, until smooth and elastic.

Put the dough into a clean bowl, cover with cling film and leave to rise in a warm place for 20 minutes. Then, on a lightly floured surface, re-knead the dough until smooth.

Cut the dough into two equal pieces and roll out each one on a lightly floured board or worksurface, to dinner plate size.

Freeze the bases for up to 4 months wrapped in cling film and then in foil.

FROZEN ASSETS

Experiment with different types of cheese. Simply omit the Cheddar and use your favourite hard cheese in its place.

100

se passata in place of
e pasta sauce, if you
refer.

Time	30 minutes plus thawing time
Calories per portion	889 Kcal
Fat per portion	39g
of which saturated	19.2g
Serves	2
Suitable for vegetarians	

Ready-made pizza base thawed at room temperature for 30–40 minutes
Olive oil for brushing
Tomato and herb pizza topping 250g jar
Red pepper ½, deseeded and cut into rings
Green pepper ½, deseeded and cut into rings
Spring onions 6, trimmed, halved and cut into strips
Sun-dried tomatoes in olive oil 4–6, drained and roughly chopped
Mature Cheddar cheese 75g (3oz), coarsely grated
Mozzarella 150g (5oz), thinly sliced
Basil leaves finely shredded for garnish

Cheddar and spring onion pizza

Preheat the oven to 220°C/Gas 7 and brush the pizza base lightly all over with olive oil and place on a baking tray, if necessary.

Spread the tomato and herb pizza topping evenly over the base and arrange the pepper rings over the sauce. Then add the spring onions and sun-dried tomatoes.

Sprinkle the cheeses over the top and then bake in the centre of the oven for 20–25 minutes until cooked and lightly browned. Scatter the basil over the top of the pizza and serve immediately.

Time	30 minutes plus thawing time
Calories per portion	1057 Kcal
Fat per portion	52g
of which saturated	22g
Serves	2

Ready-made pizza base thawed at room temperature for 30–40 minutes
Olive oil for brushing
Roasted pepper and tomato pasta sauce ¾ x 350g jar
Yellow pepper 1 small, deseeded and cut into 8 thin rings
Red pepper 1, deseeded and cut into 8 thin rings
Ready sliced pepperoni 75g (3oz)
Finely shredded basil leaves 2 tbsp
Mozzarella 250g (9oz), drained and cut into thin slices
Anchovy fillets 50g can, drained (optional)
Black olives 8 (optional)

Pepperoni pizza

Preheat the oven to 220°C/Gas 7 and brush the pizza base lightly all over with olive oil and place on a baking tray.

Spread the pasta sauce evenly over the base and arrange the pepper rings and pepperoni over the sauce. Then scatter the basil over the top, followed by the mozzarella slices.

Bake the pizza in the oven for 20–25 minutes until cooked and lightly browned. Remove from oven, arrange the anchovy fillets and olives on top, if using, and serve immediately, cut into slices.

FROZEN ASSETS

Time	25 minutes
Makes sauce for 2 separate dishes	
Suitable for freezing	

Butter 25g (1oz)
Onion 1 medium, peeled and chopped
Celery 2 sticks, sliced
Skinless chicken breasts 4, cubed
Button mushrooms 150g (5oz), wiped and sliced
Plain flour 4 level tbsp
Boiling water 300ml (½ pint)
Milk 150ml (¼ pint)
Chicken stock cube 1, crumbled
Salt and freshly ground black pepper

Chicken and mushroom sauce

Make this delicious sauce in advance to use for two real classics.

Melt the butter in a saucepan. Add the onion and celery and cook over a medium heat for 3–5 minutes, until softened.

Add the chicken and mushrooms and continue to cook over a medium heat for a further 3–5 minutes, or until the surfaces of the chicken have all turned white.

Add the flour to the pan and then gradually add the boiling water and then the milk, stirring well to give a smooth sauce. Bring the sauce to the boil. Stir in the stock cube and seasoning and then simmer the sauce for 5 minutes. Remove from the hob and leave to cool.

When cold, transfer the sauce into two freezer-proof containers, cover, label and freeze for up to 3 months.

If you are unable to buy ready-rolled pastry, use ½ x 375g packet puff pastry.

Time	30 minutes plus thawing time
Calories per portion	690 Kcal
Fat per portion	40g
of which saturated	16.4g
Makes	2 pies

Chicken and mushroom sauce
1 portion, thawed at room temperature for 4–6 hours or overnight in the fridge
Ready-rolled puff pastry ½ x 375g packet
Egg 1, beaten

Chicken and mushroom pie

Preheat the oven to 220°C/Gas 7.

Unroll the pastry, cut it in half and trim so the dimensions are 1cm (½in) larger all around than the dishes you are serving the pies in. Place the rectangles on a baking sheet. Score the top of the pastry in a criss-cross pattern and then brush some egg glaze over the top.

Place the baking sheet in the oven and bake for 15 minutes, or until the pastry has risen and is a golden colour. Then remove from the oven.

Meanwhile, place the chicken and mushroom mixture in a pan and heat it through. If the mixture is still slightly frozen, heat it gently until all the ice crystals melt.

Divide the chicken and mushroom sauce between two small ovenproof dishes with a capacity of about 500ml (18fl oz) and put a rectangle of pastry on top of each. Press the pastry down lightly so it is in contact with the sauce. Place the dishes in the oven for about 5 minutes, until piping hot. Remove from the oven and serve immediately.

o make this a really quick
omplete meal, use rice
at you can cook in the
icrowave.

Time	15 minutes plus thawing time
Calories per portion	306 Kcal
Fat per portion	10g
of which saturated	4.6g
Serves	2

Chicken and mushroom sauce
1 portion, thawed at room temperature for 4–6 hours or overnight in the fridge
Basmati rice 150g (5oz), rinsed
Tikka curry paste 1 tbsp
Baby spinach ½ x 250g bag

Chicken and spinach curry

Place the chicken and mushroom mixture in a pan and heat it through. If the mixture is still slightly frozen, heat it gently until all the ice crystals melt.

Bring a pan of lightly salted water to the boil and add the rice. Turn down the heat, cover and leave to simmer for 10 minutes, until the rice is just cooked. Rinse in a sieve with boiling water.

Meanwhile, increase the heat for the chicken pan and bring the mixture to the boil. Add the tikka curry paste and cook for 2–3 minutes, then add the spinach to the pan and stir until it wilts into the curry.

Serve the curry on a bed of rice.

Time	30 minutes
Makes enough gravy for 2 separate dishes	
Suitable for freezing	

Butter 25g (1oz)
Olive oil 1 tbsp
Onions 3, peeled, halved and finely sliced (you can use a food processor for this, which is both faster and kinder to your eyes!)
Light soft brown sugar 1 tsp
Flour about 50g (2oz)
Beef consommé 2 x 415g cans
Salt and freshly ground black pepper

Onion gravy

Homemade onion gravy is really delicious, but carefully stir the onions so they are caramelised and sweet.

In a large heavy based pan, melt the butter and oil over a medium heat until the butter is foaming. Add the onions and mix well in the hot butter.

Turn down the heat, cover the pan and cook gently for 10 minutes, stirring every now and then. Add the sugar, increase the heat and cook for a further 10–15 minutes, until golden. Watch the mix and stir often enough to make sure the onions do not stick to the pan and burn.

When the onions are a golden colour, remove the pan from the heat, sprinkle in the flour and mix well (the amount of flour you use will depend on how thick you like your gravy). Gradually add the beef consommé and keep mixing until the gravy is smooth.

Return the pan to the heat once again and bring slowly to the boil, stirring all the time, then simmer for a couple of minutes or until thickened. Season to taste. Remove from the hob and leave to cool.

When cold, transfer the gravy into two freezer-proof containers, cover, label and freeze for up to 1 month.

FROZEN ASSETS

If you don't like the rich nutty flavour of Gruyère cheese, then use Cheddar instead.

104

...or an even richer mash,
...se 50g (2oz) of freshly
...rated Parmesan instead
...f Cheddar cheese.

Time	30 minutes plus thawing time
Calories per portion	527 Kcal
Fat per portion	32.5g
of which saturated	1.2g
Serves	4

Onion gravy 1 portion, thawed at room temperature for 6 hours or overnight in the fridge
Pork sausages 4–6
Potatoes such as King Edward 600g (1lb 6oz), peeled and cut into small chunks
Butter 50g (2oz)
Strong mature Cheddar cheese 75g (3oz), grated
Milk 150ml (¼ pint)
Salt and freshly ground black pepper

Sausages with mash and onion gravy

Preheat the oven to 200°C/Gas 6 and cook the sausages in a roasting tin for about 25 minutes, turning half way through, or according to packet instructions.

Meanwhile, put the potatoes in a saucepan, cover with water, add some salt and then bring to the boil. Reduce the heat and let the potatoes simmer gently for about 20 minutes until tender.

Tip the onion gravy into a pan, bring slowly to the boil and then simmer for 3–5 minutes, stirring.

When the potatoes are cooked, drain them, return to the pan and place over a low heat to get rid of any moisture. Mash and then gradually beat in the butter, cheese and milk until you have a soft but creamy mashed potato. Season well.

Serve the sausages and mash with the onion gravy and some peas.

Time	30 minutes plus thawing time
Calories per portion	181 Kcal
Fat per portion	8.6g
of which saturated	4.5g
Serves	4

Onion gravy 1 portion, thawed at room temperature for 6 hours or overnight in the fridge
French baguette 4 slices
Gruyère cheese 50g (2oz), grated
Chopped parsley to serve

French onion soup

Tip the onion gravy into a pan, bring slowly to the boil and then let it simmer for 3–5 minutes, stirring.

Meanwhile, preheat the grill to hot and toast the slices of baguette on both sides until just golden.

Liberally scatter the toasted bread with a generous amount of grated cheese on one side and grill until the cheese is melted. Then remove from the heat.

Ladle the onion soup into warm bowls and top each with two slices of cheesy toast. Garnish with chopped parsley and serve.

FROZEN ASSETS

Time	30 minutes
Makes	8 pancakes
Suitable for vegetarians, depending on the filling	
Suitable for freezing	

Plain flour 110g (4oz)
Salt a pinch
Egg 1
Whole milk 300ml (½ pint)
Butter 25g (1oz), melted

Pancakes

Yes, you can buy ready-made pancakes – but you can't beat those you make yourself.

Sift the flour and salt into a mixing bowl, make a well in the centre and add the egg and a little of the milk. Whisk slowly with a rotary or hand-held electric whisk until the mixture starts to thicken.

Gradually whisk in all the remaining milk and half of the melted butter. Cover and leave to stand for 10–15 minutes.

Heat a 20cm (8in) heavy based pancake pan or frying pan and have ready ten sheets of kitchen paper and a large plate.

Lightly wipe the pan with a little of the melted butter. Then pour a small ladle-full of the batter into the pan and quickly swirl it over the base until it is evenly coated, pouring any excess back into the batter.

Cook the pancake for approximately 30 seconds, until lightly browned underneath and the top looks almost dry. Then quickly flip, or turn the pancake over, and cook the other side until lightly browned.

Place a sheet of kitchen paper on the plate, slide the pancake out of the pan onto the paper, and then cover with another sheet of paper. Make seven more pancakes in the same way and leave to cool.

When cold, transfer the pancakes onto another plate, removing the kitchen paper and replacing it with sheets of non-stick baking paper. Over-wrap with cling film or foil and freeze for up to 4 months.

These pancakes taste good with any stir-fry sauce. Also, try with pork instead of chicken.

Time	20 minutes plus thawing time
Calories per portion	593 Kcal
Fat per portion	29g
of which saturated	8.4g
Serves	2

Ready-made pancakes 4, thawed at room temperature for 15–20 minutes
Olive oil 3 tbsp
Skinless chicken breasts 250–275g (9–10oz), cut into thin strips
Vegetable and bean sprout stir-fry mixture 300g (11oz)
Straight-to-wok sweet and sour stir-fry sauce 160g jar

Chinese-style pancakes

20

Preheat the oven to 180°C/Gas 4. Remove the cling film or foil from the pancakes and place them on a large plate still interleaved with non-stick baking paper. Cover with foil and then heat them through in the oven for about 10 minutes.

Meanwhile, make the filling. Heat 2 tablespoons of the oil in a large frying pan or wok, then add the chicken strips and stir-fry for 5–6 minutes, until cooked and opaque inside.

Add the remaining oil to the pan and then the stir-fry mixture and cook for a further 3–4 minutes, or until the vegetables are tender. Then, mix in the stir-fry sauce and heat through until piping hot.

Spoon the chicken mixture into the centre of each pancake and bring two sides in and over the filling. Then fold the top and bottom sides in and over each other. Carefully transfer onto hot plates and serve.

*his also tastes really good
ith apple slices and a
ash of brandy.*

Time	20 minutes plus thawing time
Calories per portion	457 Kcal
Fat per portion	27g
of which saturated	16g
Serves	2
Suitable for vegetarians	

Unsalted butter 40g (1½oz)
Lemon 1, finely grated zest and strained juice
Caster sugar 25g (1oz)
Ready-made pancakes 4, thawed at room temperature for 15–20 minutes
Strawberries 175g (6oz), hulled and cut into slices
Amaretto (or orange liqueur or kirsch) 2 tbsp, optional
Whipped cream or ice cream to serve

Strawberry and Amaretto pancakes

20

Put the butter, lemon zest and juice and sugar into a large non-stick frying pan and heat gently until the butter and sugar have dissolved and the mixture is piping hot.

One at a time, put the pancakes into the lemon sauce and heat through. Fold in half in the pan, and then in half again to make a triangle. Transfer onto warmed plates.

Add the strawberries to the pan and heat through in the remaining butter mixture until hot and slightly softened.

Gently stir the Amaretto (or other liqueur), if using, into the strawberries and heat through. Then spoon the strawberries and pan juices over the pancakes and serve with dollops of cream or ice cream.

Time	25 minutes
Makes enough sauce for 2 separate dishes	
Suitable for vegetarians, depending on usage	
Suitable for freezing	

Red plums 600g (1lb 6oz), halved, stoned and quartered
Ground cinnamon ¼–½ tsp
Golden caster sugar 75g (3oz)
Orange juice 3–6 tbsp

Spiced plums

Use these spiced plums as part of a stir-fry with pork or blend them and fold into whipped cream.

Tip the plums into a large heavy based pan with all the other ingredients (the amount of orange juice you use will depend on how ripe the plums are) and mix well.

Cook over a gentle heat for 8–10 minutes, stirring often. It is important to keep the heat very low or the cinnamon will burn and taste bitter.

Cook for a further 5 minutes if necessary. The exact cooking time will depend on the ripeness of the plums – you want the mix to be tender but not mushy. Then remove the pan from the heat and leave to cool.

When cold, transfer the mixture into two freezer-proof containers, cover, label and freeze for up to 1 month.

FROZEN ASSETS

You can also use the plum semi-freddo as a filling for four meringue nests.

Time	15 minutes plus thawing time
Calories per portion	713 Kcal
Fat per portion	16g
of which saturated	2.7g
Serves	3

Spiced plums 1 portion, thawed at room temperature for 3–4 hours or overnight in the fridge
Red wine vinegar 1–2 tbsp
Pork loin steaks 2, trimmed and cut into thin slices
Sesame oil 1 tbsp
Fresh egg noodles 385g packet
Oriental stir-fry mix 270g packet

•u can easily buy sesame I in supermarkets – it Ids a lovely flavour.

Stir-fry pork with spiced plum sauce

Stir together the plum sauce and vinegar and then add the strips of pork.

Heat the sesame oil in a large wok and add the pork and plum sauce – watch out, it will sizzle a bit! Stir-fry for 5–7 minutes or until the liquid from the plums has almost evaporated.

Add the remaining ingredients and stir-fry for a further 3–5 minutes or until the vegetables have wilted and the pork is cooked through. Serve at once with soy sauce, if wished.

Time	10 minutes
Calories per portion	250 Kcal
Fat per portion	20g
of which saturated	11.3g
Serves	4
Suitable for vegetarians	

Spiced plums 1 portion, still frozen
Double cream 150ml (¼ pint), lightly whipped

Plum semi-freddo

Take the plums from the freezer and remove the lid from the storage container. Microwave on high for about 10 seconds just so that you can get the plum mix out of the container.

Break the sauce into chunks and pop in a food processor. Then use the pulse button to cut the sauce into chunks.

Quickly add the chunks of sauce to the whipped cream and mix gently. Serve immediately in glasses with dessert biscuits.

Time	25 minutes
Makes enough sauce for 2 separate dishes	
Suitable for vegetarians	
Suitable for freezing	

Cox's apples about 2kg (4lb 7oz), peeled, cored and cut into chunks
Light soft brown sugar 1–2 tbsp (optional)
Orange juice 4 tbsp

Stewed apple

Take advantage of apples when they are in season – use this yummy apple base to make into a crumble or for a delicious apple cake dessert.

Tip all the ingredients into a large, heavy based pan and mix well. Cover the pan and cook for 8–10 minutes, turning every now and then, until tender. You may need to continue cooking the apples for a further 5 minutes or so. The apples should be tender but still hold their shape. Leave to cool.

When cold, transfer the mixture into two freezer-proof containers, cover, label and freeze for up to 1 month.

25

Try making the sponge with ginger or allspice instead of cinnamon.

Time	30 minutes plus thawing time
Calories per portion	424 Kcal
Fat per portion	23g
of which saturated	9.4g
Serves	4–6
Suitable for vegetarians	

Apple sauce 1 portion, thawed at room temperature for 3–4 hours or overnight in the fridge
Butter 100g (3½oz)
Light soft brown sugar 110g (4oz)
Plain flour 100g (3½oz)
Ground almonds 100g (3½oz)

Apple crumble

30

Preheat the oven to 190°C/Gas 5. Place the apple sauce in a heatproof dish suitable for a crumble (about 1.25 litres/2 pints).

To make the topping, tip the butter, sugar, flour and almonds into a food processor and press the pulse button several times until the mixture looks like fine bread crumbs. Alternatively, tip into a bowl and mix together with your fingertips.

Sprinkle the crumble over the apples and bake in the oven for 20 minutes, until golden. Serve hot, warm or cold with clotted cream or custard.

For speedy defrosting, heat the sauce in the microwave on high for 2 mins, stir, cook again for 2 mins and leave for 5 mins.

Time	30 minutes plus thawing time
Calories per portion	443 Kcal
Fat per portion	25g
of which saturated	14.3g
Serves	8
Suitable for vegetarians	

Apple sauce 1 portion, thawed at room temperature for 3–4 hours or overnight in the fridge
Self-raising flour 225g (8oz)
Ground cinnamon ½ tsp
Light soft brown sugar 125g (4½oz)
Butter 125g (4½oz), softened
Eggs 2, beaten
Double cream 150ml (¼ pint), whipped

Cinnamon sponge with apple cream

30

Preheat the oven to 200°C/Gas 6 and line a 27 x 21cm (10½ x 8¼in) baking tin with foil. Weigh 225g (8oz) of the apple sauce into a bowl and set the rest aside for later.

To make the cake mix, tip the flour, cinnamon, sugar and butter into a bowl of a food processor and blend until the mix forms large crumbs. Alternatively, tip into a bowl and mix together with your fingertips.

Add the 225g (8oz) of apple sauce and eggs and blend until smooth (using a hand-held electric whisk if you are not using a processor). Spoon into the prepared tin and bake for 20–25 minutes or until firm and springy to the touch.

Meanwhile, purée the remaining apple in a food procesor and stir into the whipped cream. Cover and chill until required.

Remove the cake from the oven, cut into eight portions and serve it while it is still hot with the apple cream.

Time	30 minutes
Makes	32 squares
Suitable for vegetarians	
Suitable for freezing	

Butter 175g (6oz), softened
Caster sugar 175g (6oz)
Eggs 3
Self-raising flour 225g (8oz)
Baking powder 2 tsp
Lemon ½, grated zest and juice

Lemon tray bake

Cook this tray bake and enjoy it dusted with icing sugar straight away, and freeze the rest for a tea time treat or as the base of a lemon and red fruit summer trifle.

Preheat the oven to 180°C/Gas 4 and grease and line with greaseproof paper a 18 x 28cm (7 x 11in) baking tin.

Put all the ingredients in the bowl of a large electric mixer (or use a hand-held electric mixer and mixing bowl) and turn on slowly so they don't splash out. Gradually increase the speed and beat until you have a smooth, pale and creamy cake batter.

Spoon into the prepared tin and bake in the oven for 25–30 minutes, until well risen and cooked. Leave to cool for 5 minutes before removing from the tin.

Cut the cake in two. Then trim the edges of one half and cut into six squares. Dust four of the squares with icing sugar and serve as a tea-time treat or leave plain and serve for a pudding treat in school lunch boxes.

Separately open freeze the remaining half and two squares of the cake on wire racks until firm. When firm, wrap in cling film and freeze for up to 1 month.

To speed up the thawing, pop the tray bake on a microwave-proof plate and thaw on defrost for 3–5 minutes.

30

FROZEN ASSETS

112

Time	15 minutes plus thawing time
Calories per portion	700 Kcal
Fat per portion	52.1g
of which saturated	2.7g
Serves	2
Suitable for vegetarians	

Lemon tray bake 2 squares, loosely covered on a wire rack to thaw at room temperature for 1–2 hours
Limoncello liqueur 2 tbsp
Frozen summer fruit 175g (6oz), just defrosted
Custard 150g tub
Double cream 125ml (4fl oz), lightly whipped
Crystallised rose petals to decorate

Last-minute summer trifle

Crumble the cake squares into the bottom of two glass tumblers. Add 1 tablespoon of liqueur to each and divide the summer fruits over the top.

Spoon over the custard and then the cream. Chill until ready to serve.

Decorate the top of the trifles with crystallised rose petals.

r a change, substitute
e lemon curd with
ange curd, which is also
ailable in most large
permarkets.

Time	15 minutes plus thawing time
Calories per square	412 Kcal
Fat per square	28.8g
of which saturated	1.4g
Makes	6 squares
Suitable for vegetarians	

Lemon tray bake ½, loosely covered on a wire rack to thaw at room temperature for 3–4 hours
Double cream 150ml (¼ pint)
Luxury lemon curd 75g (3oz)
Raspberries or other fresh fruit to decorate

Iced lemon squares

Pop the thawed cake on a board and trim the edges. Whip the cream until thick and then fold in the lemon curd.

Cut the cake into six squares, split them across the middle and fill and top with the cream and lemon curd mix.

Decorate with raspberries or a selection of fresh fruit and serve at once.

Side orders

You'll find that these delicious extras won't be left on the side for long.

For speedy and thin cucumber slices, use the slicing attachment on your food processor.

Time	25 minutes
Calories per portion	76 Kcal
Fat per portion	6g
of which saturated	0.8g
Serves	2
Suitable for vegetarians	

Cucumber 1 piece weighing about 200g (7oz)
Sea salt for sprinkling
Mild red chilli ½–1, deseeded and finely chopped
Chopped mint 2 tbsp, plus extra to garnish
Olive oil 1 tbsp
White wine vinegar 2 tbsp
Clear honey 2 tsp

Spicy pickled cucumber salad

This quickly pickled salad is perfect for serving with pan-fried salmon.

Trim the cucumber and cut into very thin slices (see above). Arrange the slices in a sieve and sprinkle with salt. Leave for 10 minutes and then rinse the cucumber slices. Drain thoroughly and tip into a serving dish.

Mix together all the remaining ingredients to make a dressing and pour over the prepared cucumber. Leave the salad to stand for 10 minutes for the flavours to infuse and serve garnished with the remaining chopped mint.

Time	10 minutes
Calories per portion	227 Kcal
Fat per portion	17.7g
of which saturated	2.9g
Serves	4
Suitable for vegetarians	

Watercress 50g (2oz), stalks removed
Wild rocket 50g (2oz)
Baby leaf spinach 50g (2oz)
Carrot 1 large, peeled and grated
Cherry tomatoes 150g (5oz), halved
Red pepper 1 small, deseeded and
thinly sliced
Canned chickpeas 100g (3½oz),
drained
Sunflower seeds 2 tbsp, lightly toasted

For the avocado dressing
Avocado 1
Dijon mustard 1 tsp
Lemon juice 2 tbsp
Tabasco sauce dash of
Olive oil 2 tbsp

Chickpea, tomato and red pepper salad with avocado dressing

This salad can be served as a simple lunch, a side dish or alongside griddled chicken fillets, lean ham or tuna.

Mix together the leaves and carrot and divide between four plates or one serving platter. Tuck the tomato halves and pepper slices among the leaves and scatter over the chickpeas and seeds.

To make the avocado dressing, halve the avocado and remove the stone. Scoop the flesh into the smallest bowl of a food processor and add the mustard, lemon juice and Tabasco sauce.

Blend until smooth, and then, with the motor still running, gradually pour in the oil and 2–3 tablespoons of warm water. If you don't have a food processor, mash the avocado, oil and warm water with a fork. Season to taste.

Drizzle the dressing over the salad and serve.

SIDE ORDERS

10

For an alternative dressing, mix 2 teaspoons Dijon mustard, 1 teaspoon white or red wine vinegar and 3 tablespoons olive oil until very thick. Add water, if necessary, and season.

Time	15 minutes
Calories per portion	117 Kcal
Fat per portion	7g
of which saturated	0.8g
Serves	4
Suitable for vegetarians	

Carrot 1, peeled, scrubbed and grated
Chickpeas ½ x 410g can, rinsed and drained
Sultanas 25g (1oz)
Olive oil 1 tbsp
Toasted sesame oil 1 tbsp
Spring onions 2, trimmed and chopped
Ground cumin ¼ tsp
Fresh orange juice 2 tbsp
Clear honey ½ tsp
Chopped coriander 2 tbsp
Salt and freshly ground black pepper

Make houmous with leftover chickpeas by blending with garlic, lemon juice and a dash of sesame and olive oils.

Sunshine salad

It is so easy to serve up the same old salads, but try this quick little number – it tastes great and looks wonderful.

Tip the grated carrot and chickpeas in a bowl with the sultanas and mix together well.

Heat the oil in a small frying pan and gently cook the spring onions and ground cumin for about a minute, taking care not to burn the spring onions or spices as it will ruin the flavour of the salad.

Add the hot spice mix to the grated carrots and mix well. Then add the remaining ingredients and season to taste.

SIDE ORDERS

Celeriac and swede are very hard root vegetables, so take extra care when removing the peel – and make sure the knife is sharp.

Time	20 minutes
Calories per portion	84 Kcal
Fat per portion	1g
of which saturated	0g
Serves	2
Suitable for vegetarians	

Carrot 1, peeled and coarsely shredded or grated
Celeriac 125g (4½oz) piece, peeled and coarsely shredded or grated
Swede 75g (3oz) piece, peeled and coarsely shredded or grated
Parsnip ½, peeled and coarsely shredded or grated
Honey 1 tsp
Seasoned rice vinegar, white or red wine vinegar 1 tbsp
Wholegrain mustard 1 tsp
Chopped parsley 2 tbsp

Roots of goodness

This crisp and crunchy side salad is refreshingly delicious. Serve it with roast chicken or cold meats.

Mix the carrot, celeriac, swede and parsnip in a mixing bowl.

To make the dressing, in a small bowl whisk together the honey, vinegar, mustard and parsley.

Pour the honey dressing over the salad and mix well. Serve immediately, or cover and chill in the refrigerator until serving.

To ring the changes, try this salad with pecan nuts instead of walnuts.

SIDE ORDERS

Time	15 minutes
Calories per portion	183 Kcal
Fat per portion	14g
of which saturated	3.5g
Serves	4
Suitable for vegetarians if using a Parmesan substitute	

Fennel 2 bulbs, peeled and cut in half from top to bottom
Lemon ½, juice only
Olive oil for dressing
Sea salt
Slightly under-ripe pears 2, peeled, cored and thinly sliced
Roasted walnut pieces a handful
Parmesan cheese 50g (2oz), shaved

Pear, fennel and walnut salad

This goes well with grilled fish, but it is also delicious served on its own as a starter.

Lay the flat surface of the fennel halves on a chopping board and slice in a cross section from side to side – the pieces will be slightly harp-shaped.

Dress the fennel with the lemon juice, a glug of the oil and a generous pinch of sea salt. Set it to one side.

Add the pear slices to the fennel and toss them together so they are coated with the dressing. Top with the walnut pieces and the Parmesan shavings.

Time	25 minutes
Calories per portion	336 Kcal
Fat per portion	33g
of which saturated	4.2g
Serves	2
Suitable for vegetarians	

Artichoke antipasto in oil 280g jar, drained and 2 tbsp reserved for cooking
Small aubergine 225g (8oz), trimmed, halved and then cut roughly into 2.5cm (1in) cubes
Spring onions 2 large, trimmed and cut diagonally into 7.5cm (3in) pieces
Medium curry powder 1–2 tsp
Cherry tomatoes 8–10 depending on their size
Chopped coriander 2 tbsp

Artichokes and aubergines

This lively combination is the perfect partner for roast or grilled meat, chicken or fish.

Heat the artichoke oil in a large frying pan, preferably non-stick. Add the aubergine and gently stir-fry the aubergine for 6–8 minutes until softened and very lightly browned.

Add the artichokes and spring onions and continue cooking for 2–3 minutes until the onions are slightly softened. Stir in the curry powder and tomatoes and continue cooking for 3–4 minutes more, or until the tomatoes are hot and slightly split.

Gently mix in the coriander and serve immediately.

SIDE ORDERS

25

Artichoke antipasto is a good standby to have in the storecupboard, as it can liven up many a lack-lustre dish.

For a vegetarian version, omit the bacon, and cook the leek in a tablespoon of vegetable oil, and use vegetable stock instead of chicken.

Time	20 minutes
Calories per portion	159 Kcal
Fat per portion	7g
of which saturated	2.1g
Serves	2

Smoked streaky bacon 2 rashers, trimmed and cut into thin strips
Leek 1, trimmed, split lengthways and finely shredded
Chicken stock 300ml (½ pint)
Frozen peas 250g (9oz)
Little Gem lettuce 1, trimmed and finely shredded
Salt and freshly ground black pepper

French-style peas

When lettuce is crisp and young, it is deliciously sweet when very lightly cooked. Serve it with fish or chicken.

Put the bacon and leek in a medium-sized saucepan and dry fry for 5 minutes until the leeks have softened. Pour over the chicken stock, bring to the boil and then add the peas. Cover and cook for 5 minutes until tender.

Remove the lid and stir in the lettuce for 1 minute until just wilted. Season to taste. Traditionally this dish is served with the cooking liquid, but you can drain the peas if you prefer.

Ladle into a warm serving dish and serve while warm.

20

SIDE ORDERS

Time	30 minutes
Calories per portion	97 Kcal
Fat per portion	1g
of which saturated	0.1g
Serves	2
Suitable for vegetarians	

Beefsteak tomatoes 2 large
Spring onions 2, trimmed and
chopped
Cooked white rice 75g (3oz)
Canned kidney beans 3 tbsp
Canned sweetcorn kernels 3 tbsp
Salt and freshly ground black
pepper
Dried mixed herbs ½ tsp
Chilli powder ½–1 tsp, to taste

Chilli rice stuffed tomatoes

An all-in-one accompaniment for a classic chilli beef casserole or any grilled meats.

Preheat the oven to 220°C/Gas 7 and lightly grease a small ovenproof dish.

Slice the tops off the tomatoes and reserve. Using a grapefruit spoon or teaspoon, scoop out the seeds and flesh into a bowl and discard the seeds.

Mix the spring onions in to the tomato. Add all the remaining ingredients and mix well.

Stand the tomato shells in the prepared dish and fill each one with the rice mixture, packing down well. Sit the tomato tops back on top, cover with lightly greased foil and bake for about 25 minutes until just tender. Drain and serve.

SIDE ORDERS

30

To turn this dish into a Mexican-inspired main meal, replace the sweetcorn with chopped cooked roast beef, and add plenty of grated Parmesan cheese.

Rinsing the rice quickly before cooking ensures you end up with separate grains.

Time	25 minutes
Calories per portion	313 Kcal
Fat per portion	3.9g
of which saturated	0.5g
Serves	4
Suitable for vegetarians	

Groundnut oil 1 tbsp
Onion 1 small, peeled and finely chopped
Cinnamon stick 1, split lengthways
Cumin seeds ¾ tsp, dry-toasted in a pan and crushed
Cardamom pods 2
Cloves 6
Ground turmeric 2 tsp
Thyme a few sprigs
Bay leaves 2
Long grain rice 300g (11oz)
Boiling water 600ml (1 pint)

Pilau rice

An authentic accompaniment to home-made curries.

Heat the oil in a large pan with a tight-fitting lid. Add the onion and gently cook until it has softened. Stir in the spices and herbs and cook for 1 minute.

Add the rice and stir until coated. Add the boiling water and bring to the boil. Cover, then simmer on the lowest setting for 12–15 minutes, until tender. Let the steam dry off, then fluff up with a fork.

For the very best flavour, choose Desirée or King Edwards potatoes and steam instead of boiling to retain the flavour.

Time	15 minutes
Calories per portion	315 Kcal
Fat per portion	14g
of which saturated	7.3g
Serves	3
Suitable for vegetarians	

Potatoes 680g (1½lb), peeled and cut into slices 1.25cm (½in) thick
Butter 40g (1½oz)
Watercress 60g packet, trimmed and chopped
Chopped parsley 3 tbsp
Spring onions 4, trimmed and thinly sliced diagonally
Sun-dried tomatoes in olive oil 6, drained and roughly chopped

Mashed potatoes with attitude

Revive humble mash with some flavoursome additions.

Steam the potatoes for 15–20 minutes until cooked (a foldaway steamer basket placed in a shallow, wide lidded frying pan is ideal for this as it speeds up the cooking time). Take care not to let the potatoes over cook.

Remove the potatoes from the steamer and pour away the water. Return the potatoes to the pan and mash them well with the butter. Then mix in the watercress, parsley, spring onions and sun-dried tomatoes and serve while warm.

Time	30 minutes
Calories per portion	191 Kcal
Fat per portion	6g
of which saturated	0.8g
Serves	2
Suitable for vegetarians	

Baking potatoes 3 small
Vegetable oil 1 tbsp
Smoked paprika ½ tsp
Ground cumin ½ tsp
Dried thyme ½ tsp
Salt and freshly ground black pepper

Spiced potato wedges

A hassle-free and healthier alternative to chips to serve with kebabs, grilled meats or as a starter.

Preheat the oven to 220°C/Gas 7 and lightly grease a baking tray.

Scrub the potatoes and cut them into even-sized wedges of less than 1.5cm (²⁄₃in) thick. Put the wedges in a bowl and mix in the oil, spices and thyme, until well coated. Arrange the wedges, spaced apart, on the baking tray and season well.

Bake in the oven, turning once, for about 25 minutes until tender and golden. Drain well and serve immediately with sour cream topped with snipped chives.

SIDE ORDERS

30

Cut the potato pieces to the same thickness to ensure they cook evenly and are ready at the same time.

Desserts

Fruit has never been so tasty or attractive with these tasty treats.

The orange cups can be made at least 1 hour before serving and kept, covered, in the refrigerator.

Time	20 minutes
Calories per portion	194 Kcal
Fat per portion	14g
of which saturated	8.1g
Serves	2
Suitable for vegetarians	

Orange 1 large
Light soft brown sugar 2 tsp
Double cream 3 tbsp
Natural Greek yogurt 3 tbsp
Raspberries 6 large
Blueberries 10
Cointreau or Grand Marnier 1 tbsp (optional)

Orange cups

Creamy, rich and fruity, this Grand Marnier-laced dessert is a real treat.

Cut the orange in half widthways. Then carefully remove the segments using a small, sharp pointed knife, retaining the halved orange shells and cutting between the transparent, tissue-like membrane. Cut the segments into smaller pieces, then put into a small bowl, add the sugar and set aside.

Pull out as much of the white pith from each orange shell as is possible and remove narrow strips of orange zest from the shell with a zester. Set aside for decoration.

Put the cream and yogurt into a small bowl and whisk lightly until it just holds a trail – then gently mix in the orange segments, raspberries and blueberries.

Spoon the cream into the orange shells and put onto small serving plates. Then cover and refrigerate until serving.

Just before serving, drizzle a little of the liqueur over the creams, if using, and serve decorated with the raspberries, blueberries and pieces of orange zest.

If you are unable to find mini marshmallows, use larger ones and snip them into smaller pieces using damp scissors.

Time	10 minutes
Calories per portion	347 Kcal
Fat per portion	20g
of which saturated	11.3g
Serves	2
Suitable for vegetarians	

Strawberries 250g (9oz), hulled and quartered, reserving two whole for decoration
Double cream 75ml (2½fl oz)
Icing sugar 1 tbsp
Kirsch 1 tbsp
Pink and white mini marshmallows a few, to decorate

Strawberry marshmallow cream

This is a truly light and fluffy indulgent dessert.

Mash half the strawberries in one bowl and slice the other half.

Pour the cream into a separate bowl and add the icing sugar and kirsch. Whisk the mixture until it just forms soft peaks.

Layer the mashed strawberries with the cream and strawberry slices into two glasses or dishes. Sprinkle a few marshmallows over the top and serve immediately.

Time	25 minutes
Calories per portion	177 Kcal
Fat per portion	7g
of which saturated	3.5g
Serves	4
Suitable for vegetarians	

Banana 1, peeled and sliced
Pears 2, peeled, cored and sliced
Blueberries a handful
Orange juice 2 tbsp
Granola 75g (3oz)
Cold butter 25g (1oz), diced

Pear and banana granola crumble

Perfect miniature crumbles in minutes!

Preheat the oven to 180°C/Gas 4. Divide the banana, pears and blueberries between four 150ml (¼ pint) ramekins and drizzle over the orange juice.

Put the granola and butter in a separate bowl and use your fingers to rub the butter lightly into the granola. Sprinkle the topping over the ramekins and bake for 15–20 minutes.

Rest for 5 minutes, then serve with cream or ice cream.

25

Granola is a baked version of muesli and can be found in the cereal section of the supermarket.

Time	10 minutes
Calories per portion	159 Kcal
Fat per portion	6g
of which saturated	1.9g
Serves	2
Suitable for vegetarians	

Figs **4**
Ground cinnamon **½ tsp**
Honey **2 tbsp**
Natural Greek yogurt **4 tbsp**
Toasted flaked almonds **1 tbsp**

Honeyed figs

These sweet hot figs are wonderfully reminiscent of Mediterranean holidays.

Preheat the grill to hot. Cut the figs into quarters, without cutting all the way through. Open them out and place on a small baking tray. Sprinkle over the cinnamon and then drizzle with the honey.

Place the baking tray with the figs under the grill and cook for 3–5 minutes until the honey starts to bubble. Serve two figs on each plate with a dollop of Greek yogurt. Sprinkle over the flaked almonds and serve immediately.

Runny honey is best to use, but if using a thick honey, allow a little extra cooking time for it to go runny.

Time	25 minutes
Calories per portion	507 Kcal
Fat per portion	30g
of which saturated	17.6g
Serves	4
Suitable for vegetarians	

Butter 50g (2oz)
Rolled oats 75g (3oz)
Caster sugar 50g (2oz)
Whipping cream 150ml (¼ pint)
Natural Greek yogurt 110g (4oz)
Honey 2 tbsp
Whisky 2 tbsp
Light muscovado sugar 2 tbsp
Blackberries 200g (7oz)
Tart apples 2, such as Granny Smith,
peeled, cored and sliced
Crème de mûre or crème de cassis
to drizzle

Blackberry and apple cranachan

A boozy and fruity traditional Irish pudding.

Melt half the butter in a small pan, add the oats and cook for 1 minute, then add half the caster sugar. Stir for 4–5 minutes, until the oats are lightly caramelised, then tip onto a piece of baking paper and leave to cool.

Lightly whip the cream, then fold in the yogurt, honey, whisky, muscovado sugar and oats. Stir in the blackberries (set aside a few to decorate), crushing them slightly.

In a pan, melt the remaining butter and sauté the apples (in two batches, if necessary) for 3–4 minutes. When the apples begin to soften, add the remaining caster sugar and cook until caramelised. Set aside.

Layer up the cream and oats with the apples in four glasses or one big bowl. Top with the reserved blackberries and drizzle with a little crème de mûre or cassis. Serve with shortbread, if you like.

DESSERTS

25

You can use Bramley apples instead of Granny Smiths if you like, but dip them in sugar before sautéeing.

Choose any berries on offer in the supermarket or use frozen mixed berries, defrosted in the fridge overnight.

Time	15 minutes plus chilling
Calories per portion	368 Kcal
Fat per portion	6.4g
of which saturated	3.3g
Makes	4
Suitable for vegetarians	

Mixed berries 500g (1lb 2oz), raspberries, blueberries, redcurrants, blackberries and strawberries, chopped if large
Caster sugar 75g (3oz)
Crème de framboise or sweetened cranberry juice 4 tbsp
Brioche 16 slices, each 1cm (½in) thick
Single cream to serve

Individual summer puddings

Get the taste of summer, whatever the time of year.

Place the berries in a pan with the sugar and liqueur or cranberry juice. Heat gently until the fruits start to release their juices. Remove from the pan and tip into a sieve over a bowl to collect the juices.

With a 9cm (3½in) round cutter, cut out eight discs from the brioche. Dip into the drained juices and press four of the soaked brioche circles into the bottom of four 200ml (6½fl oz) ramekins.

Cut strips from the remaining brioche slices, dip in the juices and use to line the sides of the ramekins. Divide the berries between them and fit the four remaining brioche circles (soaked in juice) as lids on top. Cover loosely with cling film and stack, placing a small plate on top. Chill for 30 minutes or until ready to serve.

To serve, run a knife around the inside of the ramekins and tip out the puddings carefully onto plates. Drizzle with any leftover berry juices and serve with single cream.

Choose a good quality lemon curd to get a natural tasting tang to the cream filling.

Time	10 minutes
Calories per portion	194 Kcal
Fat per portion	12.6g
of which saturated	7.7g
Serves	2
Suitable for vegetarians	

Crème fraîche **3 tbsp**
Lemon curd **1 tbsp**
Ready made brandysnap baskets **2**
Raspberries **100g (3½oz)**
Icing sugar **for dusting**

Lemon and raspberry tarts

The rich and creamy filling with a citrus tang makes these tarts a most refreshing dessert.

Tip the crème fraîche into a bowl and fold in the lemon curd. Spoon the mixture into the brandysnap baskets.

Arrange the raspberries on top of the lemon cream and dust over icing sugar before serving.

You don't have to use peaches – choose plums or nectarines instead. Simply buy what is best value at the time.

25

Time	25 minutes
Calories per portion	183 Kcal
Fat per portion	7g
of which saturated	1.9g
Serves	6
Suitable for vegetarians	

Peaches 4–5, halved, stoned and peeled
Caster sugar 75g (3oz), plus extra 1–2 tbsp
Marsala, Vin Santo or Amontillado sherry 175ml (6fl oz), plus 3 tbsp
Egg 6, yolks only

Peach zabaglione

Fluffy and fruity – simply divine.

Slice the peaches into a large frying pan over a medium-high heat and sprinkle with 1–2 tablespoons of caster sugar to taste together with the 3 tablespoons of Marsala, Vin Santo or Amontillado sherry. Fry briskly for 2–3 minutes, until just tender and then spoon into six dessert glasses and set aside.

Put the egg yolks and remaining sugar into a heatproof bowl and whisk with an electric hand whisk for 5 minutes, until the mixture is thick and pale yellow.

Place the bowl over a pan of barely simmering water and whisk for 15 minutes, drizzling in a little of the remaining Marsala, Vin Santo or sherry every now and then, until the mixture almost triples in volume and is light, foamy and holding in soft peaks. Take care not to get the mixture too hot or it will start to cook. Spoon on top of the peaches and serve while still warm.

Time	25 minutes
Calories per portion	233 Kcal
Fat per portion	12g
of which saturated	6.9g
Serves	2
Suitable for vegetarians	

Nectarines 2, halved
Butter 25g (1oz), melted
Amaretti biscuits 4, crushed
Honey 1 tbsp
Lemon juice 1 tbsp

Amaretti baked nectarines

This crunchy topped fruit has just the taste of Italy.

Preheat the oven to 180°C/Gas 4.

Arrange the nectarine halves in an ovenproof dish, cut-side up. Brush some of the melted butter over the cut surfaces.

Stir the crushed amaretti biscuits, honey and lemon juice into the remaining butter and use the mixture to fill the cavities of the nectarines. Add 2 tablespoons of water to the base of the dish so the juices don't burn when cooking.

Place the dish with the nectarines in the oven and bake for about 20 minutes, or until the topping is crisp. Remove from the oven and serve immediately with crème fraîche or mascarpone.

25

Use ripe nectarines as they will be sweeter as well as softer than unripe ones.

Time	20 minutes
Calories per portion	330 Kcal
Fat per portion	17g
of which saturated	9.6g
Serves	6
Suitable for vegetarians	

Bramley apples 2, peeled, cored and chopped
Caster sugar 75g (3oz)
Lemon juice a squeeze
Toffee sauce 6 tbsp
Shortbread biscuits 6
Whipping cream 150ml (¼ pint)
Icing sugar 2 tsp
Toasted almonds to serve

Toffee apple trifle

Toffee apples and trifle – here is a grown-up version of two childhood classics.

Put the apples in a saucepan with the caster sugar and lemon juice and cook for 10 minutes until really soft. Then blitz in a food processor or mash with a fork until smooth.

Swirl the toffee sauce through the apples, divide between six individual glass bowls and crumble over the shortbread biscuits.

Whip the cream with the icing sugar and spoon over the crumbs. Top with the toasted almonds and serve.

To vary the recipe, try amaretti biscuits in place of the shortbread.

If it is cheaper, buy a supermarket own-brand version of Nutella.

DESSERTS

5

Time	5 minutes plus chilling
Calories per portion	426 Kcal
Fat per portion	27.8g
of which saturated	2.7g
Serves	4
Suitable for vegetarians	

Espresso powder 1 tsp
Nutella 250g (9oz)
Natural Greek yogurt or fromage
frais 175g (6oz)
Chopped toasted hazelnuts 2 tbsp

Nutella mousse

This is a truly scrumptious, super-quick mousse.

In a bowl, blend the espresso powder with a little hot water. Then mix in the Nutella together with the yogurt or fromage frais and the chopped hazelnuts.

Spoon into four little pots and chill. Serve with biscuits topped with apple slices and halved hazelnuts.

143

Time	15 minutes
Calories per portion	509 Kcal
Fat per portion	34g
of which saturated	18.2g
Serves	2
Suitable for vegetarians	

Dark chocolate 50g (2oz), broken into small pieces
Boiling water 4 tbsp
Fresh pineapple 2 thick slices
Double cream 90ml (3fl oz)
Your favourite liqueur such as Grand Marnier, Kirsch, Rum or Brandy
Raspberries 12
Ginger biscuits 4, crushed

Tropical ginger creams

Forget about the calories – this dessert has a large helping of 'the feel good' factor.

Put the chocolate into a small bowl, add the boiling water and stir until melted.

Using a large plain round pastry cutter (a little smaller than the pineapple slices), cut out the flesh from each slice. Then, using a small plain round pastry cutter, remove the hard woody core. Cut the pineapple into small pieces.

Pour the cream into a mixing bowl, add your chosen liqueur and whisk until the cream holds a soft, floppy peak. Then gently fold in the pineapple, taking care not to over mix, as the mixture will then be too stiff.

Spoon the cream into two large wine glasses, alternating layers of raspberries and the melted chocolate and sprinkling the crushed biscuits over the top before the final drizzle of melted chocolate. Serve immediately.

This dessert is best served immediately after making, although the biscuits and pineapple can be prepared ahead of time.

Try making this pud with another good-quality cordial such as blackcurrant.

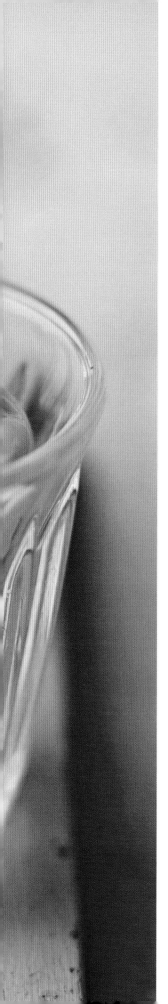

Time	5 minutes plus chilling
Calories per portion	428 Kcal
Fat per portion	40g
of which saturated	22.6g
Makes	4
Suitable for vegetarians	

Double cream 300ml (½ pint)
Elderflower cordial 3 tbsp
Icing sugar 1 tbsp
Light soft brown sugar for sprinkling
Elderberries softened in a pan with a splash of water, to serve, optional

Elderflower creams with melted soft brown sugar

An eccentrically English summer dessert.

Whip the double cream with the elderflower cordial and icing sugar until soft peaks have formed.

Spoon into glasses and sprinkle with the soft brown sugar. Chill in the fridge for 20 minutes, until the sugar has melted into the cream.

Scatter with softened elderberries, if using.

Take the biscuit

Biscuits and cakes are the perfect partner for coffee, or just a treat in themselves.

Use milk or dark chocolate chips if preferred, and replace the apricots with sultanas or glacé cherries.

Time	20 minutes plus chilling
Calories per slice	228 Kcal
Fat per slices	12g
of which saturated	6.8g
Makes	15 slices
Suitable for vegetarians	

Unsalted butter 110g (4oz)
White chocolate chips 200g (7oz)
Ginger biscuits 200g (7oz), crushed
Ready-to-eat dried apricots 200g (7oz), chopped
Mini marshmallows 75g (3oz)
Chocolate vermicelli 2 tbsp

White chocolate and apricot slice

Rich and tasty, these no-bake slices are deceptively easy and guaranteed to be popular.

Grease and line a 20cm (8in) square cake tin.

Put the butter and chocolate chips in a saucepan and heat very gently, stirring, until melted together.

Remove from the heat and stir in the biscuits, apricots and marshmallows. Press into the tin, sprinkle with the chocolate vermicelli and chill for 2 hours or until set.

Slice into 15 bars and remove from the tin to serve. Store, covered, in the fridge, for up to a week.

A great way to use up stale cake crumbs – even old Christmas cake can be transformed using this simple recipe.

Time	15 minutes plus cooling and chilling
Calories per slice	318 Kcal
Fat per slice	14g
of which saturated	8.2g
Makes	10 slices
Suitable for vegetarians	

Butter 75g (3oz)
Golden syrup 75g (3oz)
Plain cake 450g (1lb), crumbled
Cocoa powder 2 tbsp, plus 2 tsp to decorate
Glacé cherries 75g (3oz), chopped
Almond extract 1 tsp
Icing sugar 75g (3oz)
Dark chocolate small bar

No-bake chocolate cherry truffle cake

A real chocolate sensation that is sure to impress!

Line an 18cm (7in) round cake tin with a double layer of cling film.

Put the butter in a large saucepan with the syrup and heat gently until melted. Then set aside to cool for 10 minutes.

Meanwhile, put the cake crumbs in a bowl and sieve in the 2 tablespoons of cocoa powder. Stir into the crumbs along with the cherries, almond extract and the melted syrup.

Transfer to the prepared cake tin and press down evenly. Cover and chill for at least 2 hours before serving.

To make a soft chocolate icing, sieve the icing sugar and remaining cocoa powder into a bowl and stir in 2–3 teaspoons of water.

Carefully remove the cake from the tin, discard the cling film and put on a serving plate. Spread with the chocolate icing and sprinkle with chocolate curls made by running a swivel bladed vegetable peeler over the underside of the bar of chocolate. If the chocolate is too hard, microwave it for 15–20 seconds on full power and try again. As the chocolate softens, so the curls get bigger.

Allow the icing to set for about 10 minutes before cutting into eight portions to serve.

Time	20 minutes plus chilling time
Calories per square	211 Kcal
Fat per square	12.7g
of which saturated	6.6g
Makes	20 squares
Suitable for vegetarians	

Butter 125g (4½oz), chopped
Dark chocolate 300g (11oz), broken into pieces
Golden syrup 3 tbsp
Glacé cherries 100g (3½oz), halved
Pistachios 50g (2oz), roughly chopped
Sultanas 50g (2oz)
Digestive biscuits 200g pack, broken into pieces

Chocolate and pistachio fridge cake

This is really, really rich, but utterly divine.

Line a 20cm (8in) square baking tin with cling film.

Place the butter, chocolate and syrup into a large microwave-proof bowl and cook on medium for 1–2 minutes, stirring after every 20 seconds and checking the chocolate does not over heat and seize.

Add the rest of the ingredients and mix well. Spoon into the prepared tin and spread out evenly. Leave to cool. Chill for at least 1 hour or until set and then remove from the tin and peel off the cling film before cutting into squares.

It is easy to over-heat chocolate in a microwave and the times given are only a guide as the wattage of microwaves varies.

Time	25 minutes
Calories per swirl	334 Kcal
Fat per swirl	20.5g
of which saturated	13g
Makes	6–7 swirls
Suitable for vegetarians	

Unsalted butter 175g (6oz), softened
Icing sugar 50g (2oz), plus extra for dusting
Salt a pinch
Plain flour 150g (5oz)
Cornflour 2 tbsp
Seedless raspberry jam 4–5 tbsp

Raspberry swirls

These buttery sandwich biscuits will melt in the mouth.

Preheat the oven to 180°C/Gas 4 and line a baking sheet (or sheets) with baking parchment.

Place the butter in a bowl and, using a hand-held electric mixer, beat it until softened. Then add the icing sugar and salt and continue to beat until smooth.

Tip the flour and cornflour into the creamed mixture and fold it in to give a thick paste.

Fill a piping bag fitted with a star piping tube with the mixture. Pipe 12–14 5cm (2in) diameter circles of the mixture onto the lined baking sheet(s).

Bake the swirls in the centre of the oven for about 15 minutes, until they are a light golden colour.

Remove from the oven and transfer the swirls to a wire rack. Spoon a little of the jam into the centre of half of the swirls, top with the remaining biscuits and sift over some icing sugar. Serve the swirls warm or cold.

25

TAKE THE BISCUIT

To make these even more colourful, use assorted colours of jam and lemon curd in the centres.

Time	25 minutes plus cooling
Calories per cookie	72 Kcal
Fat per cookie	4g
of which saturated	0.5g
Makes	30 cookies
Suitable for vegetarians	

Porridge oats **125g (4½oz)**
Medium oatmeal **50g (2oz)**
Light soft brown sugar **110g (4oz)**
Heather honey **2 tbsp**
Vanilla extract **a few drops**
Vegetable oil **110ml (3½fl oz)**
Egg **1, beaten**

Honey flapjack cookies

Both wheat and dairy free, these little oaty crunchies are completely irresistible.

Preheat the oven to 180°C/Gas 4 and line two large baking trays with baking parchment.

Put all the ingredients in a bowl and mix well. Then put heaped teaspoonfuls of the mixture, well spaced apart, on the baking sheets and flatten slightly with the back of the spoon – you should be able to make 30 cookies.

Bake for 12–15 minutes until they are a rich golden brown. Leave them to cool for 10 minutes on the baking trays before transferring to wire racks to cool completely.

For the best results, choose a stronger tasting variety of honey and add a teaspoon of cinnamon or ground mixed spice for a different flavour.

To use up the egg whites, consider making the Shortbread with Hazelnut Topping on page 160.

Time	25 minutes
Calories per biscuit	149 Kcal
Fat per biscuit	5g
of which saturated	2.9g
Makes	15 biscuits
Suitable for vegetarians	

Raisins 50g (2oz)
Rum 1 tbsp
Glacé cherries 75g (3oz)
Unsalted butter 75g (3oz), cut into
small pieces
Dark soft brown sugar 150g (5oz)
Eggs 2, yolks only
Plain flour 175g (6oz)

Rum and raisin biscuits

Fruity, crispy and crunchy – biscuits perfect for dunking.

Preheat the oven to 180°C/Gas 4, line two baking trays with baking parchment and fit a dough blade into a food processor, if using one.

Put the raisins into a small bowl, add the rum and set aside.

Meanwhile, using scissors, cut the cherries into small pieces directly into the food processor bowl. Add the butter, sugar, egg yolks and flour, and then blend together for 1–2 minutes, or until the mixture forms a soft dough. Stir in the raisins. If you do not have a food processor, cream the butter and sugar together by hand, or with an electric hand-held mixer. Then mix in all the remaining ingredients.

Taking a small, walnut-sized piece of the rum and raisin mixture at a time, roll the dough into balls and place them, well apart, on the prepared baking trays.

Using a fork dipped in cold water, gently flatten the balls into rounds about 6cm (2½in) in diameter.

Bake for 15 minutes, or until the biscuits feel firm to the touch and are lightly browned. Remove the biscuits from the oven, allow them to cool on the trays until they feel firm and then transfer onto racks to cool completely.

If you are unable to find any dried cranberries, use raisins or sultanas in their place.

Time	25 minutes
Calories per cookie	134 Kcal
Fat per cookie	10g
of which saturated	6.2g
Makes	15 cookies
Suitable for vegetarians	

Plain flour 250g (9oz)
Ground cinnamon 1 tsp
Salt a pinch
Unsalted butter 175g (6oz)
Light soft brown sugar 75g (3oz)
Dried cranberries 150g (5oz)

Cranberry and cinnamon cookies

A rich shortbread lightly spiced with cinnamon with a contrasting tang from the dried cranberries.

Preheat the oven to 180°C/Gas 4 and grease a baking sheet.

To make the dough, sift the flour, cinnamon and salt into a bowl. Add the butter, cut into pieces, and rub it into the flour until the mixture resembles fine breadcrumbs.

Add the sugar to the bowl and continue to work the mixture until it starts to bind together. Add the dried cranberries and work the mixture to form a dough.

Roll the dough into a sausage shape about 7cm (2¾in) diameter and cut into slices about 1cm (½in) thick and place them on the baking sheets.

Bake the cookies in the centre of the oven for 15–20 minutes, until they are starting to turn light golden in colour. Remove from the oven and leave them to cool on the tray for a few minutes, then transfer to a wire rack to cool. Serve the biscuits warm or cold.

25

Time	30 minutes
Calories per slice	352 Kcal
Fat per slice	19g
of which saturated	10.7g
Makes	8 slices
Suitable for vegetarians	

Plain flour 175g (6oz)
Unsalted butter 110g (4oz), cut into small cubes
Caster sugar 175g (6oz)
Eggs 2, whites only
Chopped, toasted hazelnuts 40g (1½ oz)
Desiccated coconut 50g (2oz)
Raspberry jam 2 rounded tbsp

Shortbread with hazelnut topping

*Buttery shortbread topped with raspberry conserve and a
hazelnut meringue topping that just melts in the mouth.*

Preheat the oven to 180°C/Gas 4 and fit a dough blade into a food processor,
if using one.

To make the shortbread, put the flour, butter and 50g (2oz) of the sugar into
a food processor and blend for 1–2 minutes until the mixture forms a soft
dough. If you do not have a food processor, cream the butter and sugar by
hand, or with a hand-held electric mixer. Mix in the flour.

Put the dough into a non-stick, 20 x 4.5cm (8 x 1¾in) diameter springform
or loose-bottomed sandwich cake tin. Press the dough evenly across the
bottom of the tin, smoothing it out with the back of a spoon and pricking
evenly all over with a fork. Bake in the oven for 15 minutes.

Meanwhile, to make the topping, whisk the egg whites with a hand-held
electric mixer until stiff and then gradually whisk in the remaining sugar to
form a stiff, shiny meringue. Gently fold in the hazelnuts and coconut.

Remove the shortbread from the oven. Spread the jam over it and then the
meringue. Return to the oven for 10 minutes until lightly browned. Allow the
shortbread to cool and then cover and keep refrigerated until using.

When ready to serve, gently run a palette knife around the side, place the
tin on a bowl or cake tin (a little smaller than the baking tin) and gently pull
down the outer ring to release the shortbread.

The Rum and Raisin Biscuits on page 157 use egg yolks only, so you may want to make those biscuits as well.

If you don't have a deep fat fryer, use a large saucepan. Never leave it unattended.

Time	25 minutes
Calories per ring	200 Kcal
Fat per ring	7.2g
of which saturated	1g
Makes	8–10 rings
Suitable for vegetarians	

Vegetable oil **for the deep fat fryer**
Self-raising flour 250g (9oz)
Baking powder 1 tsp
Caster sugar 75g (3oz)
Egg 1 medium
Vegetable oil 1 tbsp
Milk 90ml (3fl oz)

For the coating
Ground cinnamon 1 tsp
Caster sugar 50g (2oz)

Cinnamon doughnut rings

Crisp on the outside and soft in the middle, serve these doughnuts warm as a treat or with ice cream for a dessert.

Heat the oil in the deep fat fryer to 170°C.

Meanwhile, sift the flour and baking powder into a bowl and stir in the sugar. Beat the egg and oil into the milk and add to the dry ingredients, beating with a spoon to bind them together. With floured hands, work the ingredients into a smooth ball and turn out onto a floured worksurface.

Roll out the dough to a thickness of just over 1cm (½in). Flour 7cm (2½in) and 3cm (1½in) plain round cutters and use the larger cutter to cut out rounds of dough and then cut out the centres using the smaller cutter. Re-roll the trimmings and cut more rings as necessary. Mix the cinnamon into the sugar in a small bowl for coating the doughnuts.

Cook the doughnut rings 2–3 at a time. Lower them carefully into the hot oil and cook for 3–4 minutes until golden on the bottom and then turn over and cook for a further 2–3 minutes, until they are an even golden colour and cooked through.

Lift onto kitchen paper to drain briefly and while they are still hot dip them in the cinnamon sugar and turn them over so they are evenly coated, shaking off any excess. Place on a wire rack to cool.

Time	25 minutes
Calories per scone	177 Kcal
Fat per scone	3g
of which saturated	1.9g
Makes	12 scones
Suitable for vegetarians	
Suitable for freezing	

Stem ginger 50g (2oz), chopped
Ready-to-eat prunes 75g (3oz), chopped
Self-raising flour 175g (6oz)
Baking powder 1 tbsp
Wholemeal flour 175g (6oz)
Salt a good pinch
Dark soft brown sugar 75g (3oz)
Butter 40g (1½oz), cut into small pieces
Buttermilk or natural yogurt 200ml (7fl oz)

Brown sugar, ginger and prune scones

Dainty scones made with chopped ginger and prunes – just perfect for a cosy afternoon tea by the fire.

Preheat the oven to 220°C/Gas 7, lightly dust a baking tray or two with flour and fit a dough blade into a food processor, if using one.

Add all of the ingredients to the food processor and blend for 1–2 minutes until mixed to a soft, yet slightly sticky dough. If you don't have a processor, put the dry ingredients into a bowl and use your fingertips to rub in the butter. Once the consistency of fine breadcrumbs, add the buttermilk or yogurt and bring together to form a soft, slightly sticky dough.

Turn the dough onto a lightly floured board or worksurface, knead gently for 1 minute and then roll it out to approximately 2.5cm (1in) thick. Using a 5cm (2in) plain round cutter, stamp out as many rounds as you can and place them well apart on the baking tray(s).

Gently re-knead the trimmings, re-roll and cut out more rounds – repeating until the dough is used up.

Lightly brush the top of the scones with a little milk and then bake for 12–15 minutes, or until well risen and lightly browned and sound hollow when tapped on the bottom. Cool the scones on wire racks, then serve with apricot jam and a little clotted cream if wished.

25

Try different ready-to-eat dried fruits in place of the prunes; choose your favourite.

Time	30 minutes
Calories per pastry	281 Kcal
Fat per pastry	18g
of which saturated	6.1g
Makes	8 pastries
Suitable for vegetarians	

Ready-rolled puff pastry 425g packet
Egg 1, beaten
Apple sauce 8 tsp
Golden marzipan 110g (4oz)
Apricot jam 2 tbsp, warmed and sieved
Flaked almonds 15g (½oz), toasted

Easy peasy Danish pastries

A super-speedy way to enjoy an indulgent breakfast or coffee-time snack.

Preheat the oven to 220°C/Gas 7 and line a large baking tray with baking parchment.

Unroll the pastry and cut into eight equal-sized squares. Brush each with beaten egg and then add 1 teaspoon of apple sauce on to the centre of each.

Form the marzipan into a sausage-shape about 5cm (2in) long and slice into eight. Lay a piece on top of the apple sauce on each of the pastry squares.

Fold up the corners of the puff pastry squares to meet in the middle over the marzipan, forming a mitre shape. Pinch each of the corners to seal.

Transfer to the baking tray, brush the top of the pastries with more egg and cook for 15–18 minutes until risen and golden.

Transfer to a wire rack, lightly brush with the sieved jam and sprinkle with a few almonds. They are best served warm.

Use the same cooking method, but vary the fillings, such as canned fruit, jam or squares of chocolate.

If you don't have a banana to hand, try this recipe with the same weight of frozen raspberries or blueberries – don't let them thaw.

Time	30 minutes
Calories per muffin	235 Kcal
Fat per muffin	9g
of which saturated	5.5g
Makes	12–14 muffins
Suitable for vegetarians	

Self-raising flour 300g (11oz)
Baking powder 1 tsp
Bicarbonate of soda ½ tsp
Ground cinnamon ½ tsp
Demerara sugar 200g (7oz)
Full fat milk 300ml (½ pint)
Butter 125g (4½oz), melted
Eggs 2
Peeled bananas 200g (7oz) (about 2), finely chopped

Banana and cinnamon muffins

These store cupboard muffins are a great standby for a breakfast or afternoon treat.

Preheat the oven to 200°C/Gas 6 and line 12–14 muffin-tin holes with paper cases.

Sift together all the dry ingredients, except the sugar, into a bowl. Add the sugar and mix.

Whisk together the milk, melted butter and eggs. Stir in the chopped banana. Gently fold the liquid into the dry ingredients, taking care not to over mix.

Divide the batter between the muffin cases and bake for 15–20 minutes or until well risen and golden. Serve warm.

Check on the internet for some great mail order cake decorating suppliers who stock coloured paper cases and dainty iced flowers to decorate these cakes for a very special occasion.

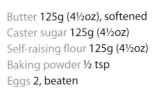

Time	25 minutes
Calories per cake	180 Kcal
Fat per cake	10.2g
of which saturated	6.1g
Makes	18 cakes
Suitable for vegetarians	
Suitable for freezing without the icing	

Butter 125g (4½oz), softened
Caster sugar 125g (4½oz)
Self-raising flour 125g (4½oz)
Baking powder ½ tsp
Eggs 2, beaten

For the butter icing
Butter 75g (3oz), softened
Icing sugar 150g (5oz), sifted
Orange 1, grated zest and 1 tsp juice
Sugar flowers to decorate

Orange iced cup cakes

Daintily iced buns, perfect for a girly coffee morning or tea party.

Preheat the oven to 190°C/Gas 5 and line 18 bun-tin holes with pretty paper cases.

Tip all the ingredients for the cake mix in a bowl (it is very important that the butter is at room temperature and thus softened). Using a hand-held electric whisk, mix well until the cake batter is smooth and creamy.

Divide the cake batter evenly between the bun cases. There is enough mixture to three-quarters fill each bun case, so don't over fill or the mixture will go all over the oven. Bake in the oven for 12–15 minutes or until well risen, golden and cooked. Remove from the oven, transfer to a wire rack and leave to cool.

Meanwhile, make the butter icing. Beat the butter with a hand-held electric whisk or wooden spoon and gradually beat in the icing sugar. Beat in the grated orange zest and enough orange juice to taste and give a soft but not runny consistency.

When the cakes are cold, spread the orange icing on top and decorate with sugar flowers. For a special event, pop the iced buns in a pretty tin and pipe a letter on each cake to spell Happy Birthday or Happy Christmas.

Time	25 minutes
Calories per cake	257 Kcal
Fat per cake	16.5g
of which saturated	7.6g
Makes	6–7 cakes
Suitable for vegetarians	
Suitable for freezing when un-iced	

Eggs **3**
Light soft brown sugar **75g (3oz)**
Plain flour **75g (3oz)**
Cocoa powder **15g (½oz)**
Unsalted butter **25g (1oz), melted and cooled**
Double cream **110ml (3½fl oz)**
Hazelnut spread **1 tbsp**
Rum, brandy or orange liqueur **2 tsp (optional)**
Icing sugar **for sifting**
Chocolate curls **for decorating**

Mini chocolate cakes with hazelnut, cream and rum filling

Light and creamy mini-sponge sandwich cakes.

Preheat the oven to 190°C/Gas 5 and grease and flour 12–14 bun-tin holes.

Put the eggs and sugar into a bowl and use a hand-held electric whisk (or use a food processor) to mix them together until the mixture is very thick, light and creamy and will hold a ribbon trail almost indefinitely when drizzled over the top.

Sift the flour and cocoa over the whisked mixture and then, using a large metal spoon, carefully fold them in. Then fold in the melted butter. Do not over-mix as the mixture may collapse.

Spoon the sponge mixture equally between the prepared bun tin holes and then bake for 12–15 minutes, or until firm to the touch. Remove the buns from the oven, allow them to cool a little, and then transfer onto a wire rack to cool.

Meanwhile, make the filling. Put the cream, hazelnut spread and chosen spirit, if using, into a bowl and whisk together until thickened. Cover and refrigerate until needed.

Spoon a little hazelnut cream on top of half of the cooled cakes followed by some whipped double cream. Cover with the remaining cakes, sift lightly with icing sugar and add some chocolate curls. Cover and keep refrigerated until ready to serve.

*When you are whisking together the
ingredients for the filling, take care not
to over-mix as the cream may curdle.*

Index

Previous books

The first book – The Dairy Book of Home Cookery – was published in 1968 and has been revised and reprinted several times due to its unprecedented popularity. Today Dairy Cookbooks are recognised as some of the most reliable recipe books ever written and have sold over 30 million copies.

The Dairy Book of Home Cookery

(416 pages) was last published in 1992, and contains hundreds of recipes, from how to make the perfect cheese sauce to creating an impressive soufflé. Now in its third reprint!

In recent years, seven new best-selling cookbooks have been published:

The New Dairy Cookbook
(192 pages) was published in 2001 and features 150 delicious new recipes for all occasions.

Quick & Easy Dairy Cookbook
(192 pages) was published in 2003 and has 130 tasty recipes, which can be prepared in less than 30 minutes.

Year Round Dairy Cookbook
(192 pages), published in 2005 and features 130 seasonal recipes to give the taste buds a treat the whole year round.

Around Britain Dairy Cookbook
(192 pages) was published in 2006 and contains favourite regional recipes plus new ones with a contemporary twist.

Hearty & Healthy
(192 pages) was published in 2007 and contains recipes to help you eat well, keep well and enjoy good food.

Clever Cooking for One or Two
(192 pages) was published in 2008 and contains mouthwatering recipes for one or two that are simple to prepare with no waste.

Just One Pot
(176 pages) was published in 2009 and shows you how to cook great food with less fuss. All recipes use just one pot each.

For more information and availability visit the Dairy Diary website at
www.dairydiary.co.uk

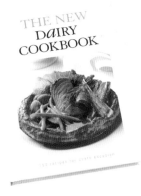

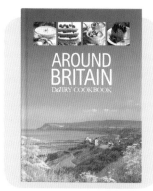